SpringerBriefs in Business Process Management

Series editor

Jan vom Brocke, Vaduz, Liechtenstein

More information about this series at http://www.springer.com/series/13170

Jens Ohlsson · Shengnan Han

Prioritising Business Processes

Design and Evaluation of the Prioritisation and Categorisation Method (PCM)

 Springer

Jens Ohlsson
Professional School
EIT Digital
Kista
Sweden

Shengnan Han
Department of Computer and Systems
   Sciences
Stockholm University
Kista
Sweden

ISSN 2197-9618   ISSN 2197-9626   (electronic)
SpringerBriefs in Business Process Management
ISBN 978-3-319-70397-8   ISBN 978-3-319-70398-5   (eBook)
https://doi.org/10.1007/978-3-319-70398-5

Library of Congress Control Number: 2017957661

Printed on acid-free paper

This Springer imprint is published by Springer Nature
The registered company is Springer International Publishing AG
The registered company address is: Gewerbestrasse 11, 6330 Cham, Switzerland

Preface

This book is an extract from the dissertation that Jens Ohlsson disputated for the Degree of Doctor of Philosophy in Computer and Systems Sciences at Stockholm University, Sweden, on 28 November 2016. The original title of the dissertation is *Exploring Designs for a Process Prioritisation Method.*

In this book, we first introduce the research problems that motivate the design of the prioritisation and categorisation method (PCM), and the design exploration process of the PCM during the years (2010–2016). We further focus on the theories that influence the design and evaluation of the PCM for supporting process prioritisation decisions. Third, we describe the PCM in detail: the process heat map (PAHM) and process categorisation map (CM), as well the way of working with the PCM in practice. The web tool of the PCM is also presented and described in steps (shown in the appendix). Fourth, we summarise the research papers that we conducted in evaluating the PCM in the two big companies in Sweden: Seco Tools and Ericsson. We then discuss the research findings and the implications for BPM research on process improvement, process prioritisation and BPM capability development. The design principles of the PCM are further articulated. We discuss the limitations and future research and make conclusions at the end.

We want to take the opportunity to thank the following people:

The Think-Tank, Duqtor, with Stefan Wernmo, Ole Schjødt-Osmo, Nevzat Ertan and Jörgen Clevensjö. Cecilia Anneroth at Ericsson for her engagement and contribution with the cases at Ericsson. Fredrik Carpenhall at Seco Tools for his engagement and contribution with the case at Seco Tools. Professor Peter Händel at Royal Institute of Technology (KTH) and the Team behind Movelo. Our colleagues at the Department of Computer and Systems Sciences, Stockholm University, especially Prof. Paul Johannesson, Prof. Lazar Rusu and Associate Prof. Ilia Bider. We would also thank Prof. Harry Bouwman from Technology University of Delft, the Netherlands, for his advice and support in this research process.

The First Applied Research Workshop series (chaired by Jens Ohlsson, 2011–2012) at the Department of Computer and Systems Sciences (DSV) at Stockholm University, with the following participants: Nevzat Ertan, Chief Enterprise Architect and Manager at the Sandvik Group; Jörgen Hansson,

Enterprise Architect at Sandvik Group; Ole Schjodt Osmo, President Process Improvement and IT Strategy at Statkraft Norge; Erik Leppenän, CIO at SSAB; Hans Narvström, Corporate CIO at Scania; Mats Högberg, Corporate CIO at Atlas Copco; Joss Delissen, Corporate CIO at Posten; Claes Wallner, Corporate CIO at Vattenfall; Fredrik Strandlund, CIO at Västerås Stad; Tomas Åkerlind, Nordic CIO at Bombardier; Johan Sundberg, CIO at Siemens Industrial Machinery; Fredrik Carpenhall, CIO/COO at SECO Tools; Stefan Wernmo, former V. P. CIO, Business Development Manager at Sandvik Tooling 2001–2011; and Björn Rosengren from Stockholm University, DSV.

The Second Applied Research Workshop series (chaired by Jens Ohlsson, 2012–2013) at the Department of Computer and Systems Sciences (DSV) at Stockholm University, with the following participants: Anders Candel, CIO at Tele2; Daniel Karlsson, CIO at Transportstyrelsen; Johan Wirf, CIO at Swedish Match; Ingo Paas, Director Corporate IT Innovation & Digitalization, ICA Group; Karin Bogen, CIO at Assa Abloy; Mats Hultin, CIO at Saabgroup; Mattias Wessman, CIO at Euromaint; Per Brandt, CIO at Munters; Per Lundqvist, COO at Cramo; and Tomas Wiik, CIO at JM, and the founders of the Think-Tank Stefan Wernmo, Ole Schjødt-Osmo, Nevzat Ertan and Jörgen Hansson and Björn Rosengren.

The Third Applied Research Workshop series (chaired by Jens Ohlsson, 2013) at the Department of Computer and Systems Sciences (DSV) at Stockholm University, with the following participants: Björn Wetterling, CIO at IFSworld; Cecilia Anneroth, Head of Business Process Support at Ericsson; Johan Bergsten, Chief Architect at SSAB; Leif Höök, Business Area Manager IT at Försäkringskassan; Lena Bornholm, Verksamhetsutvecklare at Försäkringskassan; Mats Lindeberg, CIO at Alfalaval; Michael Åsman, Head of IT Strategy and Portfolio Management at Lantmännen; Rolf Rönnback, Business and IT Architect at Apoteken Service; and Stefan Johansson, Quality, Compliance and Security Lead at Astra Zeneca, and the founders of the Think-Tank Stefan Wernmo, Ole Schjødt-Osmo, Nevzat Ertan and Jörgen Hansson and Björn Rosengren.

All of the participants in the demonstration and evaluation of the PCM at Seco Tools and Ericsson.

We would greatly thank Prof. Jan vom Brocke for encouraging and advising us to publish the book.

Kista, Sweden   Jens Ohlsson
May 2017   Shengnan Han

Contents

About the Authors

Dr. Jens Ohlsson holds Ph.D. in Computer and Systems Sciences from Stockholm University, Sweden. He is currently the Head of Professional School of EIT Digital. He is a passionate researcher, entrepreneur and business advisor. He is a well-renowned moderator and keynote speaker on digital innovations and process management. Before joining the academia, he had more than 15 years of business working experiences in big companies, e.g. SAP, IDS Scheer and a start-up innovation company Movelo AB. His research interests include business process management, disruptive technology and digital transformation. His paper has published by *Business Process Management Journal, IEEE Systems Journal, and conferences proceeding of CAiSE, PACIS, HICSS and the others.* He can be contacted by email: joelowis@gmail.com

Dr. Shengnan Han is Associate Professor of Computer and System Sciences at Stockholm University, Sweden. She received a Doctorate in Economics (information systems) from Åbo Akademi University, Finland. She is engaged in research on digital business, value-added mobile services (for business, healthcare and governments), business process management and strategic IT management. Her research has appeared in *Computers in Human Behavior, Business Process Management Journal, International Journal of Technology Assessment in Health Care, International Journal of IT/Business Alignment and Governance and International Journal of Mobile Communication,* among the others. She is on the editorial board for *Electronic Market: the International Journal on Networked Business* (Springer) and *Telematics & Informatics* (Elsevier). Her email is shengnan@dsv.su.se

Abbreviations

BPM   Business Process Management
CIO   Chief Information Officer
CM   Categorisation Map
DSR   Design Science Research
DSRM   Design Science Research Methodology
IS   Information Systems
PAHM   Process Assessment Heat Map
PCM   Prioritisation and Categorisation Method

List of Figures

List of Tables

Abstract

Process prioritisation is an ill-structured and complex problem that remains a mystery phase in business process management (BPM) research. More explorative approaches are called upon to tackle process management problems, to facilitate process innovation and to design new processes in dynamic environments. This book aims (i) to design and evaluate the prioritisation and categorisation method (PCM) for addressing process prioritisation problems and (ii) to prescribe how to design the PCM alike in an explorative approach.

This research follows the design science research (DSR) paradigm. The design exploration and the engaged scholarship approaches are also adapted. The demonstration and evaluation of the PCM have been conducted with case studies in large Swedish companies, i.e. Seco Tools and Ericsson.

This research has led to the design and evaluation of the PCM: a new context-aware, effective and holistic method for BPM, and targeting on supporting process prioritisation decisions.

This book contributes a novel method to explore BPM research, especially process prioritisation in a holistic, yet flexible and effective way. This research contributes design knowledge to DSR in the forms of the PCM as an invention, and the three design principles for the PCM: design by holistics, design by commitments and design by explorations. The execution of the PCM also promotes good BPM practice.

Keywords Process prioritisation · PCM · Exploration · Design science research Business process management · Systems thinking

Chapter 1
Introduction

The whole is greater than the sum of its parts.

—Aristotle

Abstract This chapter presents the research problems. Then, the methodology used towards the design of the Prioritisation and Categorisation Method is demonstrated. Following that, the contributions of the research are summarised. Finally, the disposition of the book is given.

Keywords Business process management · Explorative · Exploitative Process prioritization

1.1 Research Problems and Purposes

Business processes have been one of the core units of the analysis in information systems research for many years, but most specifically for Business Process Management (BPM) research. Organisations need to make consistent efforts for process improvements to maintain the alignment of these processes with their strategy, goals, and values, which ultimately generate competitive advantages (Porter 1980; Hammer 1990; Davenport 1993).

A fundamental activity of process improvement is prioritisation. Among the various methods that support business process improvements, especially process prioritisation, maturity models are receiving growing interests (e.g. Rosemann and de Bruin 2005). The applicability and usefulness of maturity models is limited, and maturity models in BPM are limited when it comes to providing more transparency and also a better support for adaptations to practice (Röglinger et al. 2012). Further, they are difficult to apply at a business management level in an organisation. Existing scientific approaches to prioritise process improvement initiatives have focused on the generation of revenue, regulatory or social responsibilities, or process strategy alignment (e.g. Bandara et al. 2010; Burlton 2010; Hammer 2007). They mainly provide generic descriptive information about the process performance or conditions; and they rarely prescribe how to improve the prioritised process

© The Author(s) 2018
J. Ohlsson and S. Han, *Prioritising Business Processes*, SpringerBriefs in Business Process Management, https://doi.org/10.1007/978-3-319-70398-5_1

(Burlton 2010). In addition, the users (e.g. managers and process stakeholders) of these methods rarely participate in the design process of these methods and models. More importantly, a way that these models and methods can be adapted to the managerial decision-making process has not yet been fully explored. Moreover, the motivation for strategic decisions and arguments behind the choices (decisions) made are poorly documented, often only visualisations of as-is and to-be are available. Consequently, prioritisation "remains as a 'mystery phase' in BPM research" (Bandara et al. 2010, p. 178).

In business practice, companies operate in an age of accelerating change, increasing uncertainty and growing complexity. Innovations and changing business environments create a lot of concern for large companies. There are new threats appearing on their horizon, both from their existing competitors and from new types of competitors, such as entrepreneurs or companies from other industries who are approaching their industry and value-chains with potentially disruptive technologies and innovative business models. In such dynamic environments, or high velocity markets, change becomes nonlinear or explorative (Eisenhardt and Martin 2000; Rosemann 2011, 2014; Tidd and Bessant 2009). Disruptive technologies and innovations require agile and radical changes/improvements of processes in order to embrace the innovations required to generate new business values. However, companies appear to lack the explorative BPM capabilities to meet the challenges and to address the "non-linear or explorative" problems. In business practice, as experienced by managers, it is difficult to prioritise among process improvement initiatives (Ohlsson et al. 2014a). It is also difficult to justify prioritisation decisions among managers in the organisation, as decisions are mostly politically driven which means that executives of business units, that are more influential, get funding for projects regardless of their contributions to business strategy and values.

Rosemann (2014) has strongly argued that the research community needs to adapt to more explorative approaches to promote the uptake of BPM in business (not only in IT). Rosemann further articulates that an explorative BPM research effort should facilitate process innovation and design new processes that can utilise disruptive technologies and satisfy a digital-savvy customer base. The key capabilities of explorative BPM are to craft process visions by involving relevant stakeholders, customers, and employees to explore how to make a desired future state; and to identify the opportunities that create new business and revenue. Furthermore, contextual factors and business contingencies should be embedded in the development of the BPM methods (vom Brocke et al. 2016) to solve prioritisation problems in specific business settings. Obviously, this explorative approach has significant impact on how prioritisation as a mystery phase can be tackled, especially for those companies that face the challenges of disruptive technologies and operate in dynamic environments.

Therefore, this research seeks to address the complex or mysterious "process prioritisation problem" by adapting this explorative BPM approach, and contributing knowledge to business process management research. Particularly, this book aims (i) to design the Prioritisation and Categorisation Method (PCM) by involving and motivating stakeholders in the design search process; and (ii) to evaluate the PCM in which context and industry factors are considered within dynamic business environments.

1.2   Methodology: Design Science Research (DSR)

Process prioritisation is considered as a mystery in process management and decision-making (Bandara et al. 2010). Simon (1973) defines an ill-structured problem as "a problem whose structure lacks definition in some respect" (p. 181). An ill-structured problem is usually very difficult, or impossible, to solve immediately. Thus, Simon promotes "design as a problem-solving activity" (Simon 1996). In order to address the process prioritisation problem, which is an ill-structured problem, this research follows Design Science Research Methodology (DSRM) (Peffers et al. 2008), which provides the preliminary guidelines for the design and evaluation of *the Prioritisation and Categorisation Method (PCM)*.

The DSRM consists of six iterative activities (Fig. 1.1):

1. **Problem Identification and Motivation**. This activity is to identify a problem that explains why the artefact (i.e. the PCM) is beneficial and should be designed, developed, demonstrated, evaluated and finally communicated.
2. **Objectives of a Solution**. This activity is to define the objectives of the PCM, which illustrates the appropriate requirements of the PCM. The output of the activity should specify in which way the PCM solves the problem.
3. **Design and Development** (Artefact). This activity is to describe the design and development process of the PCM. The conceptualization, the operations and how to apply the PCM in practice.
4. **Demonstration**. This activity is to demonstrate how the PCM can be used in a real situation with the aim of demonstrating the utility of the artefact.
5. **Evaluation**. This activity is to evaluate the PCM in terms of utility, efficacy, and quality by conducting case studies, i.e. the case of Seco Tools and Ericsson.
6. **Communication**. This activity is to communicate the research both to an audience in academic research and business practitioners.

DSRM assumes that in the phase of problem formulation, designers can define the problem well as the starting point to search for possible solutions. Thus, the nominal process that is proposed with this methodology can be implemented in

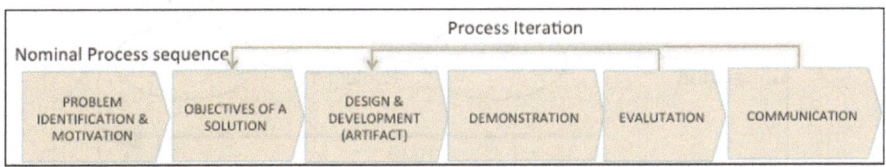

Fig. 1.1 Design science research methodology (modified from Peffers et al. 2008)

research. However, process prioritisation is an ill-structured problem, which means that the "search" process for plausible solutions is different than that of well-defined problems. Therefore, the explorative design process theorised by Maher et al. (1996) and Dorst and Cross (2001) is further adapted to reveal the design search process of the PCM.

The design process for ill-structured problems is conceptualised as "design exploration" by Maher et al. (1996). The authors elaborate that (pp. 3–4):

> Design is an iterative interplay to "fix" a problem from the problem space and to "search" plausible solutions from the corresponding solution space. The features and constrains in the current solution can become new criteria that lead to a redefined space, which in turn helps to generate a new design space. We call this phenomenon exploration.

Maher et al. (1996) propose and discuss a formal model of exploration (see Fig. 1.2). The model shows the interaction and co-evolution of a problem space and solution space. The problem space is illustrated by *P*, and the solution space is depicted by *S*. Exploration (horizontal movement) is conceptualised as a phenomenon in design where P interplays and evolves with S over time. The diagonal movement is a search process where the goals lead to a solution. This could be that the problem leads to or "fits" into the solution (downward arrow), or the solution refocuses the problem (upward arrow).

Dorst and Cross (2001) adapt and refine the co-evolution model, and suggest relevant new concepts of 'default' and 'surprise' problem/solution spaces. The authors acknowledge the significance regarding the knowledge gained in the design search process that influences the understanding of the problem space, which in turn, expands the solution space. The authors focus their study on creativity in a design process. Creativity is often characterised by the occurrence of certain significant events. If the problem is not strictly defined (ill-structured), creativity and innovation is an important element in the design exploration process. New problems arise when solutions to other problems have been made. These events can occur as sudden insights or in retrospect when thoroughly analysing results and solutions to problems identified earlier.

Simon's design theory, which respects bounded rationality, defines the discovery processes of problem solving without a goal or designing without final goals.

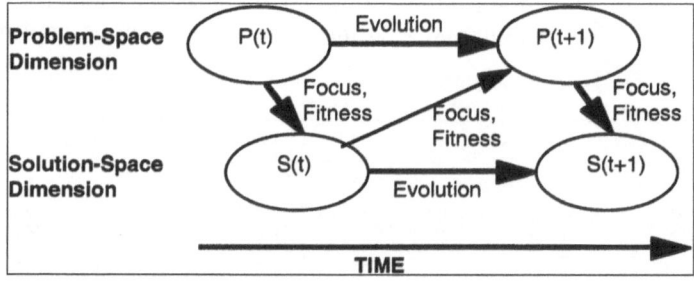

Fig. 1.2 The co-evolution model (Maher et al. 1996, p. 7)

Simon (1996, pp. 105–106) argues that:

Making discoveries belongs to the class of ill-structured problem-solving tasks that have relatively ill-defined goals. … the test that something has been discovered is that something new has emerged that could not have been predicted with certainty and that the new thing has value or interest of some kind (ibid., p. 106).

In order to increase the applicability of the PCM, the engaged scholarship approach (Van de Ven 2007) is also used to support the design by facilitating the collaboration and knowledge co-creation processes between researchers and practitioners. The engaged scholarship emphasises the importance of a highly iterative research process, where practitioners and researchers iterate problem formulations, problem solving, research design and theory building. The complementary aspect of Engaged Scholarship to DRSM is the idea that process prioritisation is an ill structured problem that is largely embedded in real organisational settings characterised by various contextual factors, politics and power struggles. To fully understand, the process prioritisation problem cannot be solely approached by researchers, and the exploration process for designing solutions becomes impossible without considering the insights, retrospect, creativity and innovation of business practitioners. In this research the problems have been continuously iterated in a co-evolution of problem spaces and solution spaces, where practitioners have been engaged in all of the research activities of the DSRM: in the problem formulations, in the designing and the development of the artefacts, in the demonstrations of the artefacts, as well as in the evaluations of them, etcetera.

Table 1.1 shows the design process and activities during the years (2010–2016). Note that these activities did not follow in a well-defined linear process as recognised in the design exploration process. Reflection and abstraction occurred throughout the design exploration process.

The data source for designing the PCM is both from the theoretical input from research and from the managers' knowledge, experience and reflections gained throughout a series of collaborative workshops (see Preface for the lists of participants). In order to create a trustworthy environment for the collaboration, we agreed with the managers that no video or audio recordings would be made. The workshop agenda, memos and learning notes are used for documenting the design process.

Case study research is a common method for evaluating designed artefacts (Hevner et al. 2004). The case study, as discussed in this thesis, adopts a qualitative, interpretive approach (Yin 2013; Eisenhardt 1989). This qualitative approach is also recommended by the BPM community to develop adaptable knowledge for practitioners (Roeser and Kern 2015). Core elements in the case studies are the complexities and insights that are gained when analysing the BPM practice, and specifically the use of the Prioritisation and Categorisation Method in process assessment and improvement projects.

The mode of data analysis is guided by the "hermeneutics" framework proposed by Cole and Avison (2007). Through the hermeneutics process, from understanding

Table 1.1 The PCM design activities and results

Timelines: research problem and solution	Main research activities and results
2010–2012 **Problem 1** CIOs' difficulties when distributing IT resources for process prioritisation purposes **Solution 1** A design of the PCM that supports the CIO's decision-making process regarding process prioritisation between IT and business	**Problem identification and motivation and defining the objectives for PCM** A collaborative research team was formed. The team included a senior researcher at the university, a senior business consultant and former CIO of a big Swedish company, a chief business architect from the same Swedish company and a vice president of process improvement and IT strategy from a Norwegian company **Design and development** The research team organised a total of five workshops, a one-day (eight hours) workshop each month, with the CIOs and senior IT/process managers from big Scandinavian companies, e.g. Atlas Copco, Postnord, Vattenfall, Västerås Stad, Bombardier Nordic, SSAB, Scania, Siemens Industrial Machinery, SECO Tools, Statkraft and Sandvik **Demonstration, evaluation and communication** The PCM was demonstrated at Seco Tools and piloted at Ericsson as case studies. A web-based application of the PCM was designed. The team consistently communicated the research to the practitioners through the workshops as well as through personal communications with other CIOs at social events throughout the three years. Other researchers at the university joined the communication activity in February 2013
2014–2016 **Problem 2** Companies have difficulties in managing processes holistically in dynamic and uncertain environments An explorative BPM is demanded in the IS research. Business contingencies and contextual factors need to be considered in developing a new method **Solution 2** Make the PCM more configurable to fit different business contexts	**Problem identification and motivation and defining the objectives for a solution** The problem was identified by the research team and the managers from Ericsson. They wanted the processes to contribute to the success of their future business **Design and development** Negotiating the process and configuring the PCM to 'fit' with Ericsson's context. The results: heat map and categorising map were configured **Demonstration, evaluation and communication** The evaluation of the eight processes using the configured PCM. Fifty-five stakeholders were interviewed and one hundred and nine process evaluations were collected. Some people were involved in the evaluation of multiple processes The core results were presented to the management board, which, within Ericsson, was called the Ericsson Steering Group (ESG) in January 2015. As a result, the ESG decided to train more stakeholders at Ericsson to use PCM Fifteen meetings with process stakeholders to calibrate the evaluation results as well as gain more insights. Materials for training more stakeholders in the use of the PCM were developed. Training on how to use the PCM was organised. Ten seminars were held involving more stakeholders/employees. Comments on the PCM delivered during seminars were documented. And two additional evaluations of the PCM were carried out independently by trained Ericsson employees. The results of these evaluations were included in the case data

via explanation to interpretation, both the managers and the researchers are able to share the meaning and knowledge of prioritising processes in the design process. The final interpretation of our joint understanding is the PCM.

1.3 Contributions and Publications

This research contributes a novel method—the PCM—to explore BPM research and the associated design principles for the PCM to design science research. The PCM requires the active engagement of stakeholders, it focuses on developing dynamic BPM capabilities and embeds organisational contingencies and contextual factors in the decision-making activities regarding the business process prioritisation, improvement and management. The PCM contributes to 'good BPM practice' (vom Brocke et al. 2014). It helps companies to explore BPM in a holistic, yet easy and flexible way.

The design search process is rarely reported in design science research. The nominal process of DSRM (Design Science Research Methodology) has largely ignored the explorative evolution between a problem space and a solution space. The present research provides empirical evidence that shows the importance of the explorative design process to support while developing a more comprehensive and systematic view between problems and solutions within a specific time frame. In addition, the results from this design science research emphasise the significance of the "engaged scholarship" approach in the design collaboration between researchers and business practitioners. This, to a great extent, increases the relevance of the research, as well as the applicability of the PCM in business. Further, the research contributes the three design principles for the PCM, which are: *design by holistics, design by commitments and design by explorations*. The nascent design principles serve as a guide for others designing methods within the context of business process management.

This book consists of the following original publications:

Ohlsson, J., Han, S., Johannesson, P., Carpenhall, F., and Rusu, L. (2014a). "Prioritising business processes improvement initiatives: The Seco tools case," In Jarke, M. et al. (eds.) *Proceedings of 26th International Conference on Advanced Information Systems Engineering* (CAiSE), *Lectures Notes in Computer Science*, LNCS 8484, pp. 256–270, Springer International Publishing Switzerland.

Ohlsson, J., Han, S., Johannesson, P., and Rusu, L. (2014b). "Developing a method for prioritising business process improvement initiatives," In *Proceedings of Pacific Asian Conference on Information Systems* (PACIS), Paper 342, Association of Information Systems (AIS). https://aisel.aisnet.org/pacis2014/342

Ohlsson, J., Han, S., and Bouwman, H. (2017). "The prioritization and categorization method (PCM): an evaluation at Ericsson," *Business Process Management Journal*, (23:2), pp. 377–398.

1.4 Disposition

The reminder of this book is organized into the following chapters:

Chapter 2: Knowledge Base
It provides the important knowledge used for the design of the PCM. The previous research regarding exploitative and explorative BPM is reviewed, and special attention is paid to the method of process improvement and process prioritisation. The theoretical background regarding organisations as social systems, organisations as networks of commitments and the bounded rationality theory in decision-making, are also described and discussed.

Chapter 3: The Prioritisation and Categorisation Method-PCM
The PCM is presented in detail. The two models of the PCM, Process Assessment Heat Map (PAHM) and Categorisation Map (CM) are described. The way of working with the PCM and the supporting web-based tool are also presented.

Chapter 4: Evaluation of the PCM
This chapter presents the results from when the PCM was demonstrated to Seco Tools and the evaluation of the configured PCM at Ericsson.

Chapter 5: Discussions
This chapter summarises and discusses the contributions of the PCM to both BPM research and design science research. The implications for practice are further presented by the ten principles of good BPM practice.

Chapter 6: Conclusions
The important results are re-stated. The contributions are highlighted. The limitations and suggestions for future research are presented at the end.

References

Bandara, W., Guillemain, A., & Coogans, P. (2010). Prioritizing process improvement: an example from the Australian financial services sector. In J. vom Brocke, & M. Rosemann (Eds.), *Handbook on business process management* (Vol. 2, pp. 177–195). Berlin Heidelberg: Springer.

Burlton, R. (2010). Delivering business strategy through process management. In: J. vom Brocke, & M. Rosemann (Eds.), *Handbook on business process management* (Vol. 2, pp. 5–37). Berlin Heidelberg: Springer.

Cole, M., & Avison, D. (2007). The potential of hermeneutics in information systems research. *European Journal of Information Systems, 16*(6), 820–833.

Davenport, T. H. (1993). *Process innovation: reengineering work through information technology.* Boston, USA: Harvard Business Press.

Dorst, K., & Cross, N. (2001). Creativity in the design process: Co-evolution of problem–solution. *Design Studies, 22*(5), 425–437.

Eisenhardt, K. M. (1989). Building theories from case study research. *Academy of Management Review, 14*(4), 532–550.

Eisenhardt, K. M., & Martin, J. A. (2000). Dynamic capabilities: What are they? *Strategic Management Journal, 21*(10–11), 1105–1121.

Hammer, M. (1990). Reengineering work: Don't automate, obliterate. *Harvard Business Review, 68*(4), 104–112.

Hammer, M. (2007). The process audit. *Harvard Business Review, 85*(4), 111–123.

Hevner, A. R., March, S. T., Park, J., & Ram, S. (2004). Design science in information systems research. *MIS Quarterly, 28*(1), 75–105.

Maher, M. L., Poon, J., & Boulanger, S. (1996). Formalising design exploration as co-evolution: A combined gene approach. In J. S. Gero et al. (Eds.), *Advances in formal design methods for CAD* (pp. 3–30). Dordrecht: Springer Science & Business Media.

Ohlsson, J., Han, S., Johannesson, P., Carpenhall, F., & Rusu, L. (2014a). Prioritising business processes improvement initiatives: The Seco tools case. In M. Jarke et al. (Eds.), *Proceedings of 26th International Conference on Advanced Information Systems Engineering* (CAiSE), *Lectures Notes in Computer Science*, LNCS 8484, pp. 256–270. Switzerland: Springer International Publishing.

Peffers, K., Tuunanen, T., Rothenberger, M. A., & Chatterjee, S. (2008). A design science research methodology for information systems research. *Journal of Management Information Systems, 24*(3), 45–77.

Porter, M. E. (1980). *Competitive strategy*. New York, NY: Free Press.

Roeser, T., & Kern, E. M. (2015). Surveys in business process management—A literature review. *Business Process Management Journal, 21*(3), 692–718.

Rosemann, M. (2011). Ambidextrous business process management. Presentation slides. Available at http://www.wiwiss.fu-berlin.de/fachbereich/bwl/angeschlossene-institute/gersch/ressourcen/Ambidextrous_BPM_Rosemann_12-3-13_Handout_klein.pdf. Last accessed on October 6, 2016.

Rosemann, M. (2014). Proposals for future BPM research directions. In C. Ouyang, & J.-Y. Jung (Eds.), *Proceedings of Second Asia Pacific Business Process Management conference*, LNBIP 181 (pp. 1–15). Switzerland: Springer International Publishing.

Rosemann, M., & de Bruin, T. (2005). Towards a business process management maturity model. In *Proceedings of the 13th European Conference on Information Systems* (ECIS), pp. 521–532.

Röglinger, M., Pöppelbuß, J., & Becker, J. (2012). Maturity models in business process management. *Business Process Management Journal, 18*(2), 328–346.

Simon, H. A. (1973). The structure of ill structured problems. *Artificial Intelligence, 4*(3–4), 181–201.

Simon, H. A. (1996). *The sciences of the artificial* (3rd ed.). Cambridge, MA: MIT Press.

Tidd, J., & Bessant, J. (2009). *Managing innovation: Integrating technological, market and organizational change* (4th ed.). England: Wiley.

Van de Ven, A. H. (2007). *Engaged scholarship: A guide for organizational and social research*. Oxford, UK: Oxford University Press.

vom Brocke, J., Schmiedel, T., Recker, J., Trkman, P., Mertens, W., & Viaene, S. (2014). Ten principles of good business process management. *Business Process Management Journal, 20*(4), 530–548.

vom Brocke, J., Zelt, S., & Schmiedel, T. (2016). On the role of context in business process management. *International Journal of Information Management, 36*(3), 486–495.

Yin, R. K. (2013). *Case study research design and methods* (5th ed.). London Great Britain: Sage Publications.

Chapter 2
Knowledge Base

Abstract This chapter presents the knowledge base to the research. First, the relevant and contemporary Business Process Management theories (both exploitative and explorative BPM) and methods for process improvement and innovation are presented and discussed. Second, the theoretical understanding of systems thinking and decision-making that influences the design choice of the Prioritisation and Categorisation Method (PCM) is discussed. It gives a general systemic view and a more specific focus on organisations as social systems supported by the systems thinking. Two other approaches that influence the design of the PCM are also discussed, i.e. organisations as networks of commitments and the theory of bounded rationality in decision-making. The chapter finishes with concluding remarks and reflections by summarising the theoretical background that the PCM is built upon.

Keywords BPM · Exploitation · Exploration · Systems thinking
Social systems · Network of commitment · Bounded rationality

2.1 Business Process Management: Exploitative and Explorative Approaches

Managing business processes is a necessity for all organisations (Becker et al. 2013). In order to keep the pace with fast changing business environments, organisations must continuously regenerate strategies, goals and objectives (Saint-Onge 1996), and thus there is a continuous demand for changing and improving their business processes. The improvement of business processes involves a series of actions that are taken, to identify, analyse and improve business processes within an organisation with the purpose of meeting new goals and objectives (Harrington 1991).

Business Process Management (BPM) has rapidly evolved as a management philosophy and discipline with a specific focus on business processes (Kokkonen and Bandara 2010). BPM "combines knowledge from information technology and

© The Author(s) 2018

J. Ohlsson and S. Han, *Prioritising Business Processes*, SpringerBriefs in Business
Process Management, https://doi.org/10.1007/978-3-319-70398-5_2

knowledge from management sciences and applies this to operational business processes" (Van der Aalst 2013, p. 1). BPM is also understood as a managerial philosophy for creating a process view of management in order to maintain a corporate competitive advantage (Hammer 2010). BPM considers the continuous improvement and the fundamental innovation of business processes to ensure that the strategic goals and objectives of an organisation can be achieved (Burlton 2010). Hammer defines BPM as a comprehensive system for managing and transforming organisational operations. However, Hammer also criticises BPM by saying that it has become a topic with too much focus on software (Hammer 2010).

Harmon (2010) positions BPM as a combination of three traditions, the quality control tradition, the management tradition and the IT tradition. He also stresses that the main challenge of BPM is its position as a holistic approach that embraces all three traditions, and that there is an alignment problem between the traditions. Individuals who come from one tradition do not appreciate the other approaches, feeling that their approach is sufficient or superior (Harmon 2010). However, BPM researchers have recognised the problem and set up a research direction from exploitation to exploration (e.g. Rosemann 2014; vom Brocke et al. 2016).

2.1.1   Exploitative BPM: The Methods for Process Improvement and Prioritisation

In a literature review on the business process, Solaimani and Bouwman (2012) provide an overview of the research areas that are, generally speaking, related to Business Process Modelling (e.g. Giaglis 2001; Yu and Wright 1997; Lin et al. 2002; Recker and Rosemann 2009), Business Process Re-engineering (e.g., O'Neill and Sohal 1999; Yu and Wright 1997; Lin et al. 2002), Business Process Management (e.g. Lee and Dale 1998; Van der Aalst et al. 2003; Duffy 1994) or Business Process Automation (Kirchmer and Pantaleo 2005; Watson and Holmes 2009). Some other, less extensive, BP areas are discussed by O'Neill and Sohal (1999), including Business Process Improvement, Core Process redesign, Process Innovation, Business Process Transformation, Breakpoint Business Process Design and Business Scope Redefinition. In this thesis, we focus on Business Process Management. In the last two decades, Business Process Management (BPM) research has advanced knowledge on process innovations and process improvements (Van der Aalst 2013).

The BPM community has produced mature knowledge regarding process modelling and information technologies that support process efficiency and performance. Methods for continuous process improvements and prioritisation have traditionally been designed based on exploitative BPM (Rosemann 2014; Kohlborn et al. 2014). Porter (1980) defines an organisation as a combination of primary and supporting processes. The primary processes consist of the processes of inbound logistics, operations, outbound logistics, marketing and sales, and services; and the supporting processes include firm infrastructure, human resource management, technology development, and procurement. Hammer and Champy (1993), and Davenport (1993), argue the important role that information technology plays in re-engineering work and processes in order to increase value creation and achieve a competitive advantage. These classical research studies claim that organisations need to make consistent efforts for process improvement in order to maintain the alignment of the processes with the business strategy, goal and value, which ultimately generate competitive advantages (e.g. Harrington 1991; Davenport 1993; Trkman 2010; Dumas et al. 2013). The fundamental activity of process improvement is prioritisation (which process to be improved first) (Burlton 2010). The maturity level of the processes and BPM is often considered as an indicator for improvement. However, the models lack applicability and configurability to practitioners (Röglinger et al. 2012), and most of the maturity models lack the validation of empirical evidence (Tarhan et al. 2016). Previous research has introduced a few methods specifically for the purpose of prioritising process improvement initiatives, for example, the business value scoring method (Bandara et al. 2010), the process performance scoring method (Huxley 2003) and the value matrix of process and strategy alignment (Burlton 2010). Although there is no standardised methodology regarding process prioritisation yet, the literature shows that the prioritisation criteria focus on: (i) the strategic importance of the process; (ii) the performance of the process; and (iii) organisational readiness for process improvement, i.e. culture, people, and governance for the implementation of a new redesigned or improved process. Previous research shares certain agreements with regards to how a process can be analysed and understood (e.g. Harrington 1991; Davenport 1993; Dumas et al. 2013). Quantitative and formal methods are recommended. So the measurements for assessing the process performance in terms of time, quality, flexibility and cost, are mostly adopted in the research (e.g. Dijkman et al. 2016). However, these methods only describe the process performance and indicate what to prioritise; the information on how to improve is mostly lacking. Bandara et al. (2010) conclude that the prioritisation "remains as a 'mystery phase' in most available guidelines" (ibid, p. 178).

2.1.2 Explorative BPM: A New Direction for Research

Exploitative BPM tools, methods and IT-related software have become a commodity, which means that companies cannot depend on them to create competitive advantages. Rosemann (2011, 2014) further points out that the weaknesses of exploitative BPM have negative impact on industries exposed to disruptive technologies and an emerging new class of competitors. As a result, *explorative* BPM has been put on the research agenda as a new direction for BPM development and application in organisations (Rosemann 2011, 2014; Kohlborn et al. 2014). Explorative BPM research goes back to the core of the BPM concept that is proposed by the classical strategic management approaches to promote the uptake of

BPM within business (not only in IT), for example Hammer (1990) and Davenport (1993). Explorative BPM research and practice should facilitate process innovation and design new processes *"capitalizing on emerging technical solutions and satisfying a consumer base with increased digital literacy"* (Rosemann 2014, p. 7). Rosemann (2014) defines the two key capabilities of explorative BPM. The first is to craft process visions *"that are compelling and transformational that they motivate staff, and customers, involved to explore how to make a desired future state..."* (ibid, p. 7). And the second is to identify the opportunity points in processes that can create new business and revenue opportunities. Organisations need new explorative BPM capabilities for value creation to better meet the demands of their customers in new business environments (e.g. Lindman et al. 2016). Lehnert et al. (2016) has argued the importance of integrating organisation's BPM capability and process improvements projects. vom Brocke et al. (2016) challenge the one-size-fits-all methods used in BPM, and instead propose a framework for a context-sensitive BPM. The BPM body of knowledge is enriched by examining and assessing a broader variety of business contexts that helps practitioners to better understand the specific business context in which the BPM initiatives are applied (Niehaves et al. 2014). Niehaves and his co-authors explicitly comment further on the negative effects of the BPM maturity models on business practice, and they argue that dynamic capabilities related to embedding contingencies in a developing BPM are needed. Obviously, this new explorative approach and thinking has profound impact on how prioritisation as a mystery phase can be tackled in BPM research.

2.1.3   Six Core Elements of Strategic BPM

To ensure the correct scope of BPM and to foster a common understanding of the research area, Rosemann and vom Brocke (2010) have defined the six core elements of strategic BPM: strategic alignment, governance, method, information technology, people and culture. They claim that these six elements, and the corresponding capabilities, increase our understanding of BPM as a holistic management discipline. The six elements "make the holistic view on BPM more tangible" (ibid, p.120). This framework "has the potential to become an essential tool for such strategy and road-mapping exercises as it facilitates the task of *allocating priorities and timeframes* to the progression of the various BPM elements" (ibid, p. 119). The elements are further defined as the following:

Strategic Alignment: Strategic alignment is defined *"as the tight linkage of organisational priorities and enterprise processes enabling continual and effective action to improve business performance"* (Rosemann and vom Brocke 2010, p. 112).

Governance: BPM governance is described *"as appropriate and transparent accountability in terms of roles and responsibilities for different levels of BPM* *(portfolio, programme, project, and operations). Governance also focuses on the design of decision-making and reward processes to guide process-related actions"* (Rosemann and vom Brocke 2010, p. 113).

Methods: Methods are defined as *"the set of tools and techniques that support and enable activities along the process lifecycle and within enterprise-wide BPM initiatives"* (Rosemann and vom Brocke 2010, p. 113).

Information Technology: Rosemann and vom Brocke (2010) have mentioned that IT-based solutions are very important for BPM initiatives.

People: People are defined as *"individuals and groups who continually enhance and apply their process and process management skills and knowledge in order to improve business performance"* (Rosemann and vom Brocke 2010, p. 113).

Culture: BPM culture is described as *"the collective values and beliefs with regard to a process-centred organisation"* (Rosemann and vom Brocke 2010, p. 113).

In an interview regarding business transformation through processes, vom Brocke (in Van den Bergh et al. 2013, p. 17) further emphasises that *"these six factors are not a cookbook-they're a stimulant for embracing an all-inclusive approach towards BPM. Context sensitivity with regard to the company's current state of affairs is crucial. Each company should adjust its approach and balance the various factors in order to optimise value creation from BPM efforts."*

2.1.4 Ten Principles of Good BPM Practice

vom Brocke et al. (2014) propose the ten principles of good BPM and further articulate the importance of BPM for an organisation to become more explorative and holistic in nature. The ten principles (vom Brocke et al. 2014) are principles of organisational context-awareness; of continuity: BPM should be a continuous and permanent practice; of enablement: BPM should build new capabilities; of holism: BPM should be inclusive in scope; of institutionalisation: BPM should be embedded in the organisational structure; of involvement of all stakeholder groups; of joint understanding; of purpose, i.e. contributing to strategic value creation; of simplicity: BPM should be economical; and of technology appropriation: BPM should make opportune use of technology.

In conclusion, BPM research has developed mature knowledge regarding how to model, analyse, automate and streamline processes, which is labelled as exploitative BPM. This approach has supported companies to overcome identified problems within a process. However, the capabilities related to the exploitation have become a commodity. Therefore, more and more BPM researchers and practitioners promote an explorative approach in conducting BPM research, which is coined as "explorative BPM". Rosemman has argued the importance of this explorative approach for BPM research (e.g. Rosemann 2011, 2014; Kohlborn et al. 2014; Van de Bergh et al. 2013). Rosemann (2014) asserts that *"Explorative BPM is a significant future opportunity, and challenge, for the BPM community"* (p. 7). The

Table 2.1 Exploitative BPM versus explorative BPM (Rosemann 2011)

Exploitative BPM	Explorative BPM
Reactive	Proactive
Today's efficiency (Process model)	Tomorrow's revenue (process vision)
Problem-focused	Opportunity-focused
Exclusive (only processes)	Inclusive (business models, products, services, etc.)
Transactional innovation	Transformational innovation

explorative approach is still in its infancy. But it will generate more ambidextrous capabilities to companies (see Kohlborn et al. 2014; O'Reilly and Tushman 2013). The following table (Table 2.1) contrasts the differences between exploitative BPM and explorative BPM.

In addition to the knowledge base from the BPM research, systems thinking has influenced the design choice of the PCM, which are, organisations as social systems (Ackoff 1994), organisations as networks of commitments (Winograd and Flores 1986), and bounded rationality in decision-making (Simon 1957, 1997).

2.2   Systems Thinking

System and management sciences have been heavily influenced by the goal-seeking paradigm, so called "hard system thinking". However, most of the criticism to this paradigm has been put forward regarding its limitations for management use. The reality facing today's managers is complex and dynamic and subject to change, reducing problem situations to a form that would make them amenable to a hard system modelling that was already considered to be a difficult and unfeasible task in the early 1980s (Checkland 1981). Checkland argues that a "hard" paradigm is unable to handle complexity and to cope with a plurality of different beliefs and values, and is not of much help when it comes to politics and power games in an organisation. He has pointed out that intervening in ill-structured problem situations requires relationship maintenance that is at least as important as goal-seeking, and answering questions about what we should do is as significant as determining how to do it.

Another limitation is that hard systems thinking is unable to deal satisfactory with multiple perceptions of reality (Jackson 2003). Stakeholders normally have diverse opinions about the nature of the system that they are involved with and about its proper purpose, or as Beer puts it *system is a very subjective thing* (Beer 1979). Therefore, in the 1970s a general understanding was established that hard system thinking was not useful for more complex situations and in problem contexts that were deemed to be more pluralist and coercive in character (Jackson 2003). Soft systems methodologies related to problem contexts were created to focus on system models expressing different viewpoints so that alternative perspectives could be systematically explored, compared and contrasted. Soft system thinkers abandoned the notion that it was possible to assume easily identifiable, agreed-on goals that could be used to provide an objective account of the system and its purpose.

The "soft systems" approach suggests that complex real world problems should be discussed and analysed within the context of the problem. The participants and the complexity of the system in focus are the two primary sources in analysing the situated problem.

2.2.1 Organisations as Social Systems

Ackoff (1981) discusses the changing concept of the corporation as an organisation and how it has evolved since the industrial revolution. He defines an organisation as (1) a purposeful system that is (2) part of one or more purposeful systems, and (3) parts of which, people, have purposes of their own. The social systems view of an organisation has evolved from a mechanistic view to an organismic view and now to a social systems model.

Mechanistic models of reality conceptualise it as a machine that works with regularity directed by its internal structure and processes together with the causal laws of nature. A mechanical view is inflexible. Therefore, it can only operate effectively if its environment is static or has little effect on it. That is where it can operate as a closed system. A rapidly changing environment requires continuous adaptation and learning by organisations if they are to stay effective. Adaptation and learning require a readiness, willingness and ability to change. Mechanistically managed and structured organisations lack such abilities (Ackoff 1994).

A social system conceived as an organism has a purpose of its own. The environment for many organisations are characterised by accelerating change, increasing uncertainty and growing complexity that diminish the possibility of accurate and reliable forecasts at an increasing rate. In such an environment, the best hope for a social system lies in its ability to bring more and more of its future under its own control. Such an approach requires a model of a social system different from the mechanistic and organismic models. The social model conceptualises a social system as a part of a larger purposeful system as well as a system with purposeful parts. It focuses on both the functions of the parts in the whole, and of the whole in the larger containing system of which it is a part. Therefore, it can yield an understanding of both the behaviour of the parts and the whole.

The social system model can help to get a better understanding of an organisation. The social system model points out that the system should be viewed as a whole and cannot be divided into independent parts because the behaviour of each part and its effect on the whole depend on the behaviour of other parts. This model can reveal why it is what it is, and why it behaves the way it does.

From a systemic point of view, an organisation consists of several components inherent with certain capabilities. In the business context of today the evolution of

Fig. 2.1 Organisation as a social system

some of these components is so fast that there is a challenge for other systems to keep up with the pace, e.g. the technological capabilities are evolving at such a pace that the organisations and individual capabilities cannot change accordingly. These components can also be defined as sub-systems. In Fig. 2.1, the sub-systems are described as Individuals, Technologies, Information, Processes, Products and Services, Organisational structures, Strategies and Business Models. These sub-systems need to be coordinated and integrated to achieve business value (Ackoff 1981, 1989). Since companies today act in an age of accelerating change, increasing uncertainty and growing complexity, the demand for coordinating and integrating the sub-systems is higher than ever, and the task of coordinating and integrating the sub-systems is also more difficult than ever.

Viewing the organisation as a holistic system can also be found when Keen (1991) argues that competitive, technical, organisational, economic, and management choices and their consequences are so interdependent that they cannot be handled in isolation from one another. To be effective, business design through IT must balance the interplay among these capabilities. If you want to lead the business initiative that depends on IT, you must manage the decision process for IT, otherwise you can end up in a situation where you have delegated the important business issues to IT people.

In order to study organisations holistically, according to Ackoff (1994), it is critically important to engage with as many of the companies' stakeholders as possible in the planning process. He stresses that if you do not plan, you will be planned for by someone else, internally or externally.

Ackoff (1994) proposes interactivism as a methodology to coordinate and engage individuals' participation in planning and decision-making. This approach is based on the three operating principles: the participative principle, the principle of continuity and the holistic principle.

The *participation* principle provides the members of an organisation with the possibility to develop and acquire an understanding of the organisation. The most important reason for *continuous* planning is the fact that its principal benefit derives from engaging in it. The *holistic* principle has two parts: the principle of coordination and the principle of integration. The principle of coordination states that no part of an organisation can be planned effectively if it is planned independently of other units at the same level. The principle of integration states that planning done independently at any level of an organisation cannot be as effective as planning carried out interdependently at all levels. When the principles of coordination and integration are combined, we obtain the holistic principle, which states that the more parts of a system and levels of it that are planned for simultaneously and interdependently, the better.

2.2.2   *Organisations as Networks of Commitments*

Organisations as networks of commitments are presented in the seminal work of Winograd and Flores (1986). This approach stresses the fundamental role of language that is played in creating social actions, communications, conversations and commitments among individuals in an organisation. One important underlying theory of this approach is the speech act theory. This theory emphasises that language is a form of human social action, and speech acts create commitments. Winograd and Flores (ibid, p. 76) argue that:

> To be human is to be the kind of being that generates commitments, through speaking and listening. Without our ability to create and accept (or decline) commitments we are acting in a less than fully human way, and we are not fully using language.

Therefore, the authors suggest that this approach can guide organisation design centred around what they named as a "conversation-for-action" model that would be developed through certain speech acts. They describe a manager as a person in a position to direct actions that affect the economic, political or physical conditions of others in the organisation. That means that an essential part of all of the management work is dealing with coordination based on conversations and communication, which builds the network of commitments. The authors argue that management decision-making should focus on the problems of communication. *"that the key elements are the conversations among the affected parties and the commitment to action... **Success cannot be attributed to a decision made by a particular actor, but only to the collective performance**"* (p. 151, emphasis added).

The authors further articulate that management should create, take care of, and initiate new commitments with an organisation for assuring effective cooperative action, as well as generating a context in which an effective action can be consistently realised.

Winograd and Flores (1986) stress the importance of pre-understanding, tradition and background for the understanding of conversations.

> An individual's pre-understanding is a result of experience within a tradition. Everything we say is said against a background of that tradition, and makes sense only with respect to it (Winograd and Flores 1986, p. 74).

The authors also point out that (ibid, p. 78):

> Knowledge and understanding... arise from the individual's committed participation in mutually oriented patterns of behaviour that are embedded in a socially shared background of concerns, actions, and beliefs.

This approach emphasises the socially situated knowledge and understanding that are vital for management to create a network of commitments, and in their decision-making.

The seminal text of Winograd and Flores (1986) is largely considered as a basis for understanding language, communication, conversation, and designing new computer-based tools for training and improving an individual's participation in organisational life, e.g. planning, or decision-making (Suchman 1993). Winograd and Flores explain that:

> New tools can be designed to operate in the domain of speech acts and conversation – the one in which terms like 'reminding', 'requesting', and 'agreeing' are relevant. We will argue that this is the most fruitful domain for understanding and facilitating management (Winograd and Flores 1986, p. 144).

In their summaries of the key thoughts regarding the influence of speech acts on organisations and management, the authors argue the key ontological design principles for a system design, among others, should focus on:

(1) In creating tools, new conversations and connections are designed;
(2) Design includes the generation of new possibilities;
(3) Tools are designed to conduct the network of conversations (commitments).

2.2.3   Bounded Rationality in Management Decision-Making

Peter Drucker, as a management philosopher and communicator has defined the manager by saying *"the manager is the dynamic, life-giving element in every business"* (Drucker 2007, p. 3). The manager has two specific tasks in his work, which are: (1) "to create a true whole that is larger than the sum of its parts, a productive entity that turns out more than the sum of the resources put into it" (ibid, p. 295), and (2) "to harmonize in every decision and action the requirements of immediate and long range future" (ibid, p. 296). Langefors (1970) also emphasises that business management has two main tasks, which are: (1) to achieve suitable efficiency for units, and (2) to achieve cooperation between the units in accordance to the strategies and goals for the company. The main activity of the manager's work is management, which is always a decision-making process. Decision-making usually involves two elements, fact and value (Simon 1997). These two elements lead to the two kinds of decision-making processes, structured and judgemental (Keen and Scott Morton 1978).

Structured decision-making has been shaped by rationalistic tradition as a source of understanding. Rationalistic tradition and its orientation can be depicted in a series of steps in decision-making: (1) characterise the situation in terms of identifiable objects with well-defined properties; (2) find general rules that apply to situations in terms of those objects and properties; and (3) apply the rules logically to the situation of concern, drawing conclusions about what should be done. The rationalistic tradition is supported by the mathematical analyses of decision-making and with the behavioural analyses of human conduct. In this discipline, decision-making is regarded as the central task of management and the task is characterised as a process of information gathering and processing. Then, rational behaviour is seen as a consequence of choosing among alternatives according to an evaluation of the outcomes (Simon 1957, 1997).

Decision-making, in practice, roughly approximates this ideal as Simon points out. However, it is impossible for the behaviour of a single, isolated individual to reach any high degree of rationality. Rationality requires a complete knowledge and anticipation of consequences. Since an individual cannot obtain comprehensive knowledge, and consequences lie in the future, they can only be imperfectly anticipated, so merely "bounded rationality" can be achieved (Simon 1957).

Simon's original view of bounded rationality has three features: search for alternatives, satisficing and aspiration adaptation. This theory defines that a person makes a "good enough/satisfactory" decision among the alternatives if this decision reaches above his/her aspiration level. Simon recognises the role of intuition and judgement played in decision-making in administration and management (Simon 1997). The unstructured or judgemental decision-making has been considered as the art of management, which is dependent largely on a manger's intuitive skills, the feeling of the phenomena, tacit knowing and reflection-in-action (Schön 1983). Although the decision support systems, designed by the rationalistic tradition, cannot replace a manager's judgements and reflections in decision-making, especially in a situation characterised by uniqueness, uncertainty and complexity (Schön 1983). Accordingly, Schön argues that the design, which is aimed to create a new solution or improve a situation, should be considered as "a reflective conversation with the situation", and consider a manager's "reflection-in-action", the artistry elements in decision-making. The process is aimed for satisficing, instead of optimising. Simon (1997, p. 139) emphasises that:

Every manager needs to be able to analyse problems systematically… Every manager needs also to be able to respond to situations **rapidly, a skill that requires the cultivation of intuition and judgement** over many years of experiences and training.

Process management and process prioritisation in organisations are characterised as complex, unique and uncertain problems, thus, the design of the Prioritisation and Categorisation Method should follow the "bounded rationality" theory and be complemented by a manager's reflection-in-action in the decision-making processes.

2.3   Implications of the Knowledge Base for Designing the PCM

The design of the Prioritisation and Categorisation Method (PCM) is influenced by the knowledge base that is presented in Sects. 2.1 and 2.2. The knowledge from both an exploitative BPM and a new explorative approach serve as the departure points of the design. While the systems thinking, which are: organisations as social systems, organisations as the network of commitments and bounded rationality in decision-making, influences the design choices. The implications of the theories for designing the PCM are summarised in Table 2.2.

2.4   Summary and Reflections

Although the research studies by Rosemann (2014), vom Brocke et al. (2016) provide some directions for explorative BPM research and suggest an extension to our understanding of BPM in a more holistic and context-sensitive way, no enabling and implementable method has yet been developed. Such a method should demonstrate that an explorative approach is feasible, while at the same time providing the empirical evidence, based on real business settings, and that such a method creates more values for BPM practice and research. In this thesis, the Prioritisation and Categorisation Method (PCM) is designed and evaluated to solve the problem of process prioritisation. As we discussed, this problem is complex, ill-structured and dynamic. Both researchers and practitioners are aware of the difficulties in solving this problem.

In dynamic environments, or high velocity markets, change becomes nonlinear or explorative. In order to maintain competitive advantages, organisations need to make consistent efforts for process improvement, and this is a management responsibility. Business Process Management is multi-facetted and complex. It has different elements and capabilities that must be coordinated and integrated, elements such as strategic alignment, governance, methods, information technologies, people and culture.

Table 2.2 The implications of the theories for designing the PCM

Theories/knowledge	Implications for designing the PCM
Exploitative BPM	
Model, analyse, automate and streamline processes for achieving operational excellency	PCM should identify problems of processes that hinder their alignments with operational goals
Explorative BPM	
Being inclusive and holistic (e.g. the six factors of BPM)	PCM should support companies to investigate the interrelationships among different dynamic capabilities, business contingencies, contextual factors, business models, products, services, etc.
Being proactive and exploring process opportunity and new revenue streams	PCM should support companies to become more explorative and ambidextrous
Organisations as social systems	
The social system model points out that the system should be viewed as a whole that cannot be divided into independent parts because the behaviour of each part and its effect on the whole depend on the behaviour of other parts	PCM should be theoretically built upon the holistic approach. PCM should not focus only on IT, process modelling or methods. Strategy, governance, people and culture, together with IT and models should be considered [six core elements of strategic BPM]
Organisations are non-mechanistic they should not be conceptualised as machines that work by internal structures and processes together with the causal laws of nature	PCM should be designed as a novel "social" method for prioritising purposes
It is critically important to engage as many stakeholders as possible in interactive decision-making processes: The three operating principles: – the participative principle – the principle of continuity – the holistic principle	PCM should support interactive evaluations and common understandings PCM should facilitate continuous process evaluations based the needs of an organisation. PCM should facilitate holistic principles
Organisations as networks of commitments	
Management is centred on the "problem of communication" and "conversation for action"	PCM should facilitate the communication and conversation among the stakeholders
Pre-understanding and background is very important in making the relevant decisions Knowledge and understanding arise from a shared background of actions	PCM should support the efficient collection of information and consider any pre-understanding of contexts and units of analysis from stakeholders of an organisation PCM should facilitate shared understanding between stakeholders
Success cannot be attributed to a decision made by a particular actor, but only to the *collective performance*	PCM should improve all of the stakeholders' participation and contribution to decision-making

(continued)

Table 2.2 (continued)

Theories/knowledge	Implications for designing the PCM
Bounded Rationality in decision-making	
Bounded rationality is a satisficing process to search for a satisfactory decision. A manager's reflection-in-action plays an important role in the decision-making process	PCM should support a decision/planning process by involving the key stakeholders in collective reflection-in-action The decision generated by the PCM should be satisfactory

Business processes have different characteristics. They can be understood as a strictly formal process where the operation and the behaviour of the process can be automated by formal BPM methodologies and BPM systems. They can also be understood as adaptive, where human activities and knowledge are crucial in a process, as in high-level management work and knowledge work.

The task of prioritising and deciding on improvement initiatives is difficult. Because of this complexity, managers are limited by bounded rationality in making these type of decisions. In other words, it is hard for managers to make purely fact-based or mechanistic decisions since many of the "truths" and facts are embedded as tacit knowledge and reflections in the minds of key stakeholders in the organisation. Process selection criteria for improvement work have to consider all of the aspects of BPM, but at the same time, being relevant for managers. This makes analysing business processes both an art and a science, thus both qualitative and quantitative methods should be applied in process analysis. The majority of the existing methods and models in BPM research are quantitative in nature, such as maturity models, that aim to quantify qualitative information by, for example, staging in maturity levels. These models are also limited when it comes to applicability.

In conclusion, knowledge about BPM and BPM capabilities in an organisation can be subjective. Thus, approaches, both for doing research in the area and designing novel methods applicable for practitioners, should aim to be complementary to mechanistic methods, and capture the subjective interpretations of the "topic in scope" or "unit of analysis". In practice, the unit of analysis could be a certain business process or another part or subset of the organisation that is being analysed. In this specific research the question is how the Prioritisation and Categorisation Method can be designed in order to support managers in deciding on their process improvement initiatives and how to engage the managers, and make them participate in the process by sharing their subjective and objective interpretations in an efficient way. It is also important that such a method also engages stakeholders, and generates networks of commitments (anchoring) in the company, and at the same time collects relevant holistic information based on the stakeholders understanding regarding the unit of analysis and it's contextual (external context and internal context) capabilities.

References

Ackoff, R. L. (1981). The art and science of mess management. *Interfaces, 11*(1), 20–26.

Ackoff, R. L. (1989). From data to wisdom. *Journal of Applied Systems Analysis, 16*(1), 3–9.

Ackoff, R. L. (1994). The *democratic corporation: A radical prescription for recreating corporate America and rediscovering success*. Oxford: Oxford University Press.

Bandara, W., Guillemain, A., & Coogans, P. (2010). Prioritizing process improvement: an example from the Australian financial services sector. In J. vom Brocke & M. Rosemann (Eds.), *Handbook on business process management 2* (pp. 177–195). Berlin: Springer.

Becker, J., Kugeler, M., & Rosemann, M. (Eds.) (2013). *Process management: A guide for the design of business processes*. Berlin: Springer Science & Business Media.

Beer, S. (1979). *The heart of enterprise* (Vol. 2). John Wiley & Sons.

Burlton, R. (2010). Delivering business strategy through process management. In vom Brocke, J., & Rosemann, M. (Eds.), *Handbook on business process management 2* (pp. 5–37). Berlin: Springer.

Checkland, P. (1981). *Systems thinking, systems practice*. Hoboken: Wiley.

Davenport, T. H. (1993). *Process innovation: Reengineering work through information technology*. Brington: Harvard Business Press.

Dijkman, R., Lammers, S. V., & de Jong, A. (2016). Properties that influence business process management maturity and its effect on organizational performance. *Information Systems Frontiers, 18*(4), 717–734.

Drucker, P. F. (2007). *The practice of management*. Amsterdam: Elsevier Ltd.

Dumas, M., La Rosa, M., Mendling, J., & Reijers, H. A. (2013). *Fundamentals of business process management*. Berlin: Springer.

Duffy, D. (1994), Managing the white space (cross-functional processes). *Management*, 35–36.

Giaglis, G. M. (2001). A taxonomy of business process modeling and information systems modeling techniques. *The International Journal of Flexible Manufacturing Systems, 13*(2), 209–228.

Hammer, M. (1990). Reengineering work: Don't automate, obliterate. *Harvard Business Review, 68*(4), 104–112.

Hammer, M., & Champy, J. (1993). Reengineering the corporation: A manifesto for business revolution. *Business Horizons, 36*(5), 90–91.

Hammer, M. (2010). What is business process management? In vom Brocke, J., & Rosemann, M. (Eds.), *Handbook on business process management 1* (pp. 3–16). Berlin: Springer.

Harmon, P. (2010). The scope and evolution of business processmanagement. In vom Brocke & M. Rosemann (Eds.), *Handbook on Business Process Management 1* (pp. 37–81). Berlin: Springer.

Harrington, H. J. (1991). *Business process improvement: The breakthrough strategy for total quality, productivity, and competitiveness* (Vol. 1). New York: McGraw-Hill.

Huxley, C. (2003). *An improved method to identify critical processes*. Australia: Queensland University of Technology.

Jackson, M. (2003). Systems thinking—creative holism for managers. London: Wiley.

Keen, P. G. W (1991). *Shaping the future: Business design through information technology*. Brington: Harvard Business School Press.

Keen, P. G., & Scott, M. (1978). *Decision support systems; an organizational perspective*. Boston: Addison-Wesley Publishing Company.

Kirchmer, M., & Pantaleo, D. (2005). Business process automation: A framework for combining best and next practices for the agile organization. In D. Pantaleo & N. Pal (Eds.). *The agile enterprise* (pp. 33–48). Berlin: Springer Science & Business Media.

Kohlborn, T., Mueller, O., Poeppelbuss, J., & Roeglinger, M. (2014). Interview with Michael Rosemann on ambidextrous business process management. *Business Process Management Journal, 20*(4), 634–638.

Kokkonen, A., & Bandara, W. (2010). Expertise in business process management. In J. vom Brocke & M. Rosemann (Eds.), *Handbook on business process management 2* (pp. 401–421). Berlin: Springer.

Langefors, B. (1970). System för företagsstyrning. (in Swedish) Studentlitteratur, Lund.

Lee, L. G., & Dale, B. G. (1998). Business process management: A review and evaluation. *Business Process Management Journal, 4*(3), 214–225.

Lin, F. R., Yang, M. C., & Pai, Y. H. (2002). A generic structure for business process modeling. *Business Process Management Journal, 8*(1), 19–41.

Lehnert, M., Linhart, A., & Röglinger, M. (2016). Value-based process project portfolio management: Integrated planning of BPM capability development and process improvement. *Business Research, 9*(2), 377–419.

Lindman, M., Pennanen, K., Rothenstein, J., Scozzi, B., & Vincze, Z. (2016). The value space: How firms facilitate value creation. *Business Process Management Journal, 22*(4), 736–762.

Niehaves, B., Poeppelbuss, J., Plattfaut, R., & Becker, J. (2014). BPM capability development–a matter of contingencies. *Business Process Management Journal, 20*(1), 90–106.

O'Neill, P., & Sohal, S. S. (1999). Business process reengineering: a review of recent literature. *Technovation, 19*(9), 571–581.

O'Reilly, C. A., & Tushman, M. L. (2013). Organizational ambidexterity: Past, Present and Future. Available at October 9, 2016 http://www.hbs.edu/faculty/Publication%20Files/O'Reilly%20and%20Tushman%20AMP%20Ms%20051413_c66b0c53-5fcd-46d5-aa16-943eab6aa4a1.pdf.

Porter, M. E. (1980). *Competitive strategy.* New York, NY: Free Press.

Recker, J. C., & Rosemann, M. (2009). Teaching business process modelling: experiences and recommendations. *Communications of the Association for Information Systems, 24*(1), 379–394.

Rosemann, M. (2011). Ambidextrous business process management, presentation slides. Available at: October 6, 2016 http://www.wiwiss.fu-berlin.de/fachbereich/bwl/angeschlossene-institute/gersch/ressourcen/Ambidextrous_BPM_Rosemann_12-3-13_Handout_klein.pdf.

Rosemann, M. (2014). Proposals for future BPM research directions. In C. Ouyang & J. –Y. Jung (Eds.), *Proceedings of Second Asia Pacific Business Process Management conference*, LNBIP 181 (p. 1–15). Switzerland: Springer International Publishing.

Rosemann, M., & vom Brocke, J. (2010). The six core elements of business process management. In J. vom Brocke & M. Rosemann (Eds.), *Handbook on Business Process Management 1* (pp. 107–122). Berlin: Springer.

Röglinger, M., Pöppelbuß, J., & Becker, J. (2012). Maturity models in business process management. *Business Process Management Journal, 18*(2), 328–346.

Saint-Onge, H. (1996). Tacit knowledge the key to the strategic alignment of intellectual capital. *Strategy & Leadership, 24*(2), 10–16.

Schön, D. A. (1983). The reflective practitioner: How professionals think in action. New York: Basic Books. (Reprinted 2013).

Simon, H. A. (1957). Models of man; social and rational. London: Wiley.

Simon, H. A. (1997). Administrative behaviour (4th ed.). New York: The Free Press.

Solaimani, S., & Bouwman, H. (2012). A framework for the alignment of business model and business processes: A generic model for trans-sector innovation. *Business Process Management Journal, 18*(4), 655–679.

Suchman, L. (1993). Do categories have politics? *Computer Supported Cooperative Work (CSCW), 2*(3), 177–190.

Tarhan, A., Turetken, O., & Reijers, H. A. (2016). Business process maturity models: A systematic literature review. *Information and Software Technology, 75,* 122–134.

Trkman, P. (2010). The critical success factors of business process management. *International Journal of Information Management, 30*(2), 125–134.

Van den Bergh, J., Thijs, S., & Viaene, S. (Eds.) (2013). *Transforming through processes.* Berlin: SpringerBrief in Business Process Management, Springer.

Van der Aalst, W. M. P. (2013). Business process management: A comprehensive survey. *ISRN Software Engineering,* 1–37.

Van der Aalst, W. M. P., ter Hofstede, A. H. M., & Weske, M. (2003). Business process management: A survey, Business Process Management Conference, Lecture Notes in Computer Science, LNCS 2678 (1019), pp. 1–12. Berlin: Springer.

vom Brocke, J., Schmiedel, T., Recker, J., Trkman, P., Mertens, W., & Viaene, S. (2014). Ten principles of good business process management. *Business Process Management Journal, 20* (4), 530–548.

vom Brocke, J., Zelt, S., & Schmiedel, T. (2016). On the role of context in business process management. *International Journal of Information Management, 36*(3), 486–495.

Watson, E. F., & Holmes, K. (2009). Business process automation. In Nof, S. Y. (ed.), *Springer Handbook of Automation, Part I* (pp. 1597–1612). Berlin: Springer Science & Business Media.

Winograd, T., & Flores, F. (1986). *Understanding computers and cognition: A new foundation for design.* Boston: Addison-Wesley Publishing Company.

Yu, B., & Wright, T. (1997). Software tools supporting business process analysis and modelling. *Business Process Management Journal, 3*(2), 133–150.

Chapter 3
The Prioritisation and Categorisation Method—PCM

Abstract This chapter presents the designed artefact—the Prioritisation and Categorisation Method (PCM). The Prioritisation and Categorisation Method (PCM) consists of two models, a Process Assessment Heat Map (PAHM) and a process Categorisation Map (CM). The design rationale of the PCM is to embrace a BPM life cycle view, which implies that a continuous assessment of process characteristics is made at different stages of the process life cycle. Next, the six core elements of the BPM, as discussed in Chap. 2 are used in the assessment. In this way, the method is grounded in theory. In addition to the theoretical grounding, the method is empirically and practically grounded, eliciting the tactical knowledge and practical experience from the BPM managers and stakeholders involved by using the business concepts the managers use in everyday practice.

Keywords Process prioritisation and categorisation · Process assessment heat map Process categorisation map

3.1 Process Assessment Heat Map (PAHM)

A Process Assessment Heat Map (PAHM) has five distinct perspectives (see Table 3.1): positioning, relating, preparing, implementing and proving perspectives. The positioning perspective is aimed at assessing the alignment of the process with the business strategy, objectives and values. Strategic positioning and value configuration are approaches (e.g. Porter 1996; Treacy and Wiersema 1995; Stabell and Fjeldstad 1998) that are functional for analysing process activities and value creation. With proper positioning, companies are able to identify the degree to which the process is aligned with their business strategy, objectives and values (Hammer 2010; Versteeg and Bouwman 2006). We argue that a positioning perspective, with the help of a PAHM, helps companies to open their employees' minds to generate critical thinking about process prioritisation and to create a shared

© The Author(s) 2018
J. Ohlsson and S. Han, *Prioritising Business Processes*, SpringerBriefs in Business Process Management, https://doi.org/10.1007/978-3-319-70398-5_3

understanding of business processes and potential improvements. The relating perspective reflects the elements of culture, people and governance, and is focussed on examining opinions and roles of as well as rewards and risks for the stakeholders exposed to or involved in the process. Literature recognises the importance of people and culture within the context of BPM (Schimiedel et al. 2013). A focus on the involvement and interests of stakeholders leads to longer-lasting and stronger process improvements and improved management (Rosemann and vom Brocke 2010). The preparing perspective implies elements of method, IT, people and culture, and it is aimed at analysing the availability and quality of key resources and the capabilities necessary for process improvements, as well as the commitment of stakeholders. The implementing perspective embodies elements of governance, methods and IT, and is focused on analysing the performance of the process (interfaces within the process) that is subject to analysis and change. The proving perspective mirrors the elements of method and governance, and concentrates on the degree to which processes are appropriately monitored and measured. Therefore, it is necessary to define the proper metrics and the right KPI levels.

Table 3.1 The interactive activities with distinct PAHM perspectives and examples of questions based on the six core elements

PAHM perspectives	Sample questions
Positioning assesses the alignment of the process with the business strategy, objectives and values	How clearly has the management positioned the process role, mandate and importance in relation to the business strategy and operational business logic? Is the process well described in the management system? Are priorities and the need for improvements shared?
Relating assesses the attitudes, roles, risks and rewards of the stakeholders exposed to the process	Do stakeholders share risks and rewards among units/departments? Do stakeholders have a clear understanding of their role in the process? Are all of the key stakeholders in agreement with the process interfaces and improvement roadmap?
Preparing assesses the availability and quality of the key capabilities for improving the process	Do people have the right skills and competence? Are the necessary resources secured? Is the process change dependent on a key person? Do people commit to the process?
Implementing assesses the performance of the process that is subject to analysis	What are the stakeholders' (internal and external) perceptions about the performance? How well do the interfaces work around supporting processes? How effective is the process?
Proving assesses the degree to which the process is appropriately monitored and measured	Is the business impact of the process measured in a reliable and valid way? What is the right level for process evaluation? What are the relevant KPIs? Is there a closed feedback loop?

Table 3.1 shows the working definitions of the five perspectives and sample questions that are adapted from previous frameworks (e.g. Hammer 2007; Rosemann and vom Brocke 2010). The perspectives follow a process life cycle view, from the process identification (positioning), process redesign (relating and preparing) and process implementation (implementing), to the process monitoring (proving).

Because each organisation has its own strategy and business processes, the model allows managers to define and refine crucial aspects and questions in each perspective that are relevant to the heat map (PAHM). The motivation for this design choice is twofold. Firstly, the questions involved should motivate and engage the managers and stakeholders to provide tactical knowledge and sample experiences, which means that the questions should be directly related to their work life, experience and context. Secondly, the information included in the heat map should be focused on each relevant process and perspective, so that the prioritisation and decision-making match the organisation in question. Relevant information to complete the heat map is collected based on interviews with managers and key process stakeholders.

We adopted Hammer's (2007) colour regimes and quantitative measurement method in the heat map. If a process according to the chosen perspective is considered by the process owners and stakeholders to be eligible for improvement, red is used to indicate that the improvement potential is more than 50%. If it is considered to have an improvement potential between 20 and 50%, amber is used, and green is used if the process is considered to have less than 20% improvement potential. The heat map offers room for comments and motivations for the assessment based on the current performance and expected improvements. The colours and comments are documented. All of the assessments based on interviews are consolidated in one table (see Fig. 3.1, which shows a PAHM to analyse the

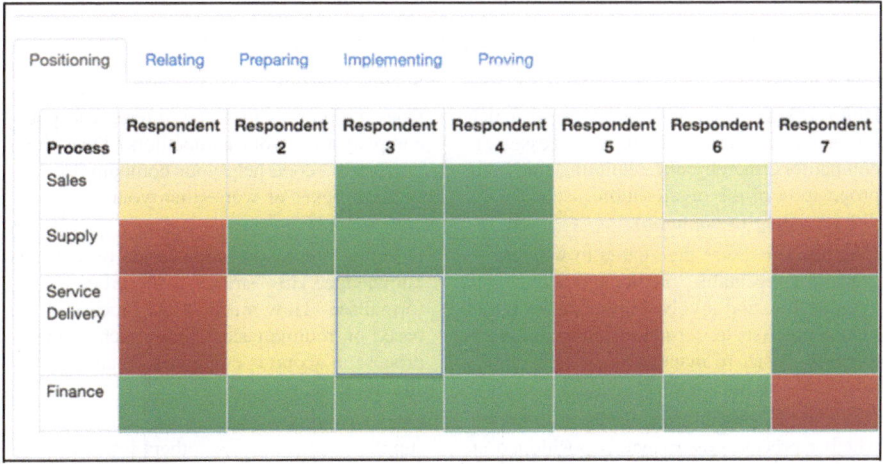

Fig. 3.1 Process Assessment Heat Map-PAHM

processes based on the answers of 7 respondents to the Positioning perspective). The process with the highest number of red assessments will be given special attention in the decision-making process facilitated by the PCM. Important complementary information for the actual decision is the qualitative data collected in conjunction with the PAHM. While, the Process Assessment Heat Map clearly shows where the priorities are. In the next step, the focus is placed on the Process Categorisation Map.

3.2   Process Categorisation Map (CM)

The Process Categorisation Map makes it possible to position processes in a space that is defined by three dimensions: differentiation, formality and governance positioning (see Table 4.2). The results are presented in what is called the Categorisation Map (CM) (see Fig. 3.2). Differentiation is the dimension to the right of the figure, formality to the left, while governance positioning is placed horizontally, A represents the current As-Is position and T the To-Be position. The map is constructed as a six-cell grid in two dimensions, rather than a cube in three dimensions, for the following reasons: (1) the results are easy to communicate using two dimensional visualisations and (2) although it is assumed that a common, informal process should not ideally exist, we realise that such a process may occur in reality and an A* is used to indicate this specific instantiation.

The map is intended to obtain indicative information on how the prioritised processes resulting from the heat map can be improved, e.g. the type of process support system that should be used, the degree of change desired, i.e. incremental *improvement or fundamental re-engineering*, and how to build a governance

Table 3.2 Categorisation Map (CM) dimensions and sample questions

CM dimensions	Sample questions
Differentiation assesses the degree to which a process is superior to similar processes of competitors, thereby differentiating the value proposition of the organisation (scale: differentiating to common)	Does the process in scope differentiate your company from your competitors? Does the process in scope help your company to perform better or worse than your competitors?
Formality assesses the degree to which a process is repeatable, predictable and automatable, and involves applications rather than people (scale: formal to informal) and is therefore easier to manage	Does the process in scope reside on tactical knowledge? How strictly is the process formalised? How much of the process is based on routine tasks? How much of the process in scope is conducted in an (un-) structured way?
Governance positioning makes it clear whether process governance is positioned at the front-end or at the back–end	Does the process under governance concern suppliers, consumers or others internal or external actors? Where is the governance of the process positioned?

Fig. 3.2 Process
Categorisation Map-CM

mechanism that is designed to create and sustain value. The dimensions for selection are based on three criteria. Firstly, the fundamental criterion for prioritising a process is the degree to which it contributes to the business strategy. Because it is important for the process to allow the company to differentiate itself from its competitors by creating added value, we define differentiation as the degree to which a process is superior to similar processes of competitors and supports the value proposition of the organisation. A continuous scale is used with processes that are core for strategic differentiation, vis-à-vis common processes.

Secondly, BPM systems have become the inseparable mirror of process management. Information technology capabilities have to support process management capabilities (Van der Aalst 2013; Mithas et al. 2011). If a process is fully aligned and supported by information technology, it can become formalised and contribute to a cost-effective execution. By contrast, if a process is unpredictable and knowledge-intensive, the operational costs will increase considerably (Swenson and Palmer 2010), which means that assessing the degree of formalisation is crucial for the analysis. Formality refers to the degree to which a process is repeatable, predictable and automatable, and it involves applications rather than people, making it easier to manage. Formality is scored on a continuous scale, with formal and informal as the extremes.

The third criterion relates to a collaboration within an internal or external organisational value configuration to co-create value for consumers, as well as for organisational units, departments or external suppliers. Revenues have to be created for every actor involved (e.g. Franz et al. 2012; Kothandaraman and Wilson 2001; Rai et al. 2012). The positioning and the role of a specific governance mechanism within the larger value creation network context helps companies to allocate limited resources, and to understand the interdependencies between internal and/or external partners (Franz et al. 2012). Understanding interdependencies leads to serious (re)consideration of where and how to structure and use governance mechanisms. Governance Positioning can be at the back-end (cost centre) or at the front-end (profit centre), which means that back-end and front-end are opposites. This distinction clearly shows where process governance mechanisms need to be positioned. For instance, if process ownership was moved from the back–end (production) to the front-end (the marketing service), the governance structure and mechanism should be transferred accordingly. The marketing manager is assigned the key accountability and responsibility related to the new process. In order to ensure the fit between business process and business environment, organisations must explicitly address the need for cross-functional collaboration, internal and external supply and demand relations, and management accountability for end-to-end business processes (Markus and Jacobson 2010).

The Categorisation Map dimensions propose the most fundamental factors for creating a process vision: business process strategy (differentiation), BPMS/IT strategy (formality) and BPM governance strategy (value network governance positioning). The operationalisation of the dimensions helps firms to incorporate these strategies into the future vision of a process. Now that we have explained the core tools for visualisation, the Process Assessment Heat Map (PAHM) and a process Categorisation Map (CM), we discuss the way they are used in practice.

3.3 The PCM Way of Working: Activities and the Web-Based Tool

When companies use the PCM to evaluate their processes, they need to: (i) create and establish a core team that will lead the evaluation and serve as interviewers, by using the Process Assessment Heat Map (PAHM) and configuring the process Categorisation Map (CM). They will fine-tune and adjust the sample questions proposed in Tables 3.1 and 3.2 in consideration of their company's business contingencies. The team will be made up of CIOs, C-level managers and senior process managers; and (ii) the team will determine the high level unit of analysis, which processes, within which business context, need to be analysed. The questions associated with the PCM need to be specified towards the business context under analysis. Next, the team selects a group of interviewees (participants) for the evaluation, the aim is (1) to involve more managers and process stakeholders (both formal and informal leaders) at different organisational levels and with different functions, in order to gather a broader array of opinions, increase visibility, transparency and the trustworthiness of the assessment, as well as to create a social and learning environment for prioritising, innovating and managing processes; (2) to ensure the quality of the data, e.g. to get reliable and valid results from the assessment.

The interview procedure is as follows. First, the interviewees are asked to decide on a colour (green, amber or red), based on their knowledge and experience of the processes in question, by interactively discussing the key questions from each perspective with the interviewers. Interviewees are expected to provide concrete arguments for choosing a specific colour. They are also asked to provide advice on how to improve the process. Next, the interviews focus on process categorisation. The interviewees perform an as-is analysis of the process by reflecting on the three dimensions and answering questions based on the current situation, after which they consider the same questions again, but with a to-be focus. The time horizon is two to three years into the future. Interviewees are asked to position the as-is dot and the to-be dot on the Categorisation Map. The interactions during the Process Assessment Heat Map help the interviewees familiarise themselves with the assessment. Their learning and reflections serve as a basis for projecting the dots onto the CM and ultimately generating the final map.

The entire process of implementing the PCM is supported by a cloud-based web tool (see Fig. 3.3, showing a summary of a specific configuration of an assessment, including selected perspectives, questions, processes (unit of analysis) and participants). The tool helps to initiate and create an assessment, select the processes to be assessed, prepare for the interviews adhering to the five PAHM perspectives and the three CM dimensions, select the participants, and document and analyse the interviews and evaluations, as well as visualise them in the PAHM (see Fig. 3.1) and CM (see Fig. 3.2).

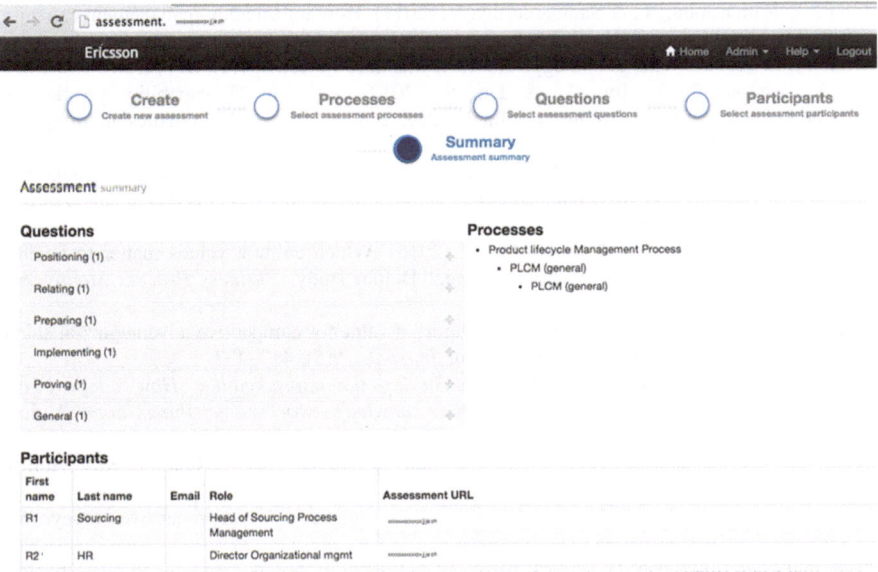

Fig. 3.3 The Prioritisation and Categorisation Method—a web based tool (manipulated screen picture)

Finally, top management can make a decision based on the aggregated results generated by the web-based tool. The PAHM supports the prioritisation of the 'red' process for improvement. The CM can help to identify the gap in the performance of the processes by comparing the different projections of the as-is dots and the to-be dots. The results generate 'coarse-grained' improvement heuristics for the to-be processes. Management can also consider aligning the core BPM elements with associated organisational capabilities in preparing the implementation of the prioritised processes, in order to realise the required changes.

The step by step description of the web-based tool for the PCM is shown in Appendix (The web-based tool for the PCM).

References

Franz, P. H., Kirchmer, M., & Rosemann, M. (2012). Value-driven business process management: Impact and benefits. *Accenture*. Available at http://www.accenture.com/SiteCollection Documents/PDF/Accenture-Value-Driven-Business-Process-Management.pdf. Last accessed on March 8, 2014.

Hammer, M. (2007). The process audit. *Harvard Business Review, 85*(4), 111–123.

Hammer, M. (2010). What is business process management? In J. vom Brocke & M. Rosemann (Eds.), *Handbook on business process management* (Vol. 1, pp. 3–16). Springer: Berlin.

Kothandaraman, P., & Wilson, D. T. (2001). The future of competition: Value creating networks. *Industrial Marketing Management, 30*(4), 379–389.

Markus, M. L., & Jacobson, D. D. (2010). Business process governance. In J. vom Brocke & M. Rosemann (Eds.), *Handbook on business process management* (Vol. 2, pp. 201–222). Springer: Berlin Heidelberg.

Mithas, S., Ramasubbu, N., & Sambamurthy, V. (2011). How information management capability influences firm performance. *MIS Quarterly, 35*(1), 237–256.

Porter, M. E. (1996). What is strategy? *Harvard Business Review, 74*(6), 61–78.

Rai, A., Pavlou, P. A., Im, G., & Du, S. (2012). Interfirm IT capability profiles and communications for cocreating relational value: Evidence from the logistics industry. *MIS Quarterly, 36*(1), 233–262.

Rosemann, M., & vom Brocke, J. (2010). The six core elements of business process management. In J. vom Brocke & M. Rosemann (Eds.), *Handbook on business process management* (Vol. 1, pp. 107–122). Springer: Berlin.

Schmiedel, T., vom Brocke, J., & Recker, J. (2013). Which cultural values matter to business process management? Results from a global Delphi study. *Business Process Management Journal, 19*(2), 292–317.

Stabell, C. B., & Fjeldstad, O. D. (1998). Configuring value for competitive advantage: On chains, shops and networks. *Strategic Management Journal, 19*(5), 413–437.

Swenson, K. D., & Palmer, N. (2010). *Mastering the unpredictable: How adaptive case management will revolutionize the way that knowledge workers get things done* (Vol. 1). Tampa: Meghan-Kiffer Press.

Treacy, M., & Wiersema, F. (1995). *The discipline of market leaders*. Reading, MA: Addison Wesley.

Van der Aalst, W. M. P. (2013). Business process management: A comprehensive survey. *ISRN Software Engineering*, 1–37.

Versteeg, G., & Bouwman, H. (2006). Business architecture: A new paradigm to relate business strategy to ICT. *Information Systems Frontiers, 8*(2), 91–102.

Chapter 4
Evaluation of the PCM

Abstract This chapter summarises the key results gained from the empirical case studies that have been conducted. These include: the demonstration of the PCM to Seco Tools (Ohlsson et al. in Prioritising business processes improvement initiatives: the Seco tools case, Springer International Publishing, Switzerland, pp 256–270, 2014a), a small scale pilot at Ericsson (Ohlsson et al. in Developing a method for prioritising business process improvement initiatives, 2014b), and the evaluation of the configured PCM at Ericsson (Ohlsson et al. in Business Process Management Journal 23(2):377–378, 2017).

Keywords PCM · Evaluation · Seco tools · Ericsson

4.1 The Demonstration of the PCM at Seco Tools

Ohlsson et al. (2014a) present the results of the demonstration of the PCM at Seco Tools, one of the large manufactory companies in Sweden.

Business context of Seco Tools

Seco Tools is a global company with approximately 5600 employees in more than 40 countries, and annual sales of 7000 MSEK ($\sim$1 BUSD) (Statistics in 2013). The company has an established reputation as a world leading manufacturer and supplier of carbide cutting tools and related equipment. Seco Tools actively contribute to improving customers' productivity and competitiveness by providing powerful machinery solutions to leading companies in the automotive, aerospace, oil and gas, energy and medical industries, among many others around the world.

Seco Tools launched "one Seco program" to improve their business processes and to achieve operational excellence in 2011. However, the senior management team did not share the same view on BPM and did not agree on how to establish a process-oriented organization. The CIO and senior vice president (VP) of process

© The Author(s) 2018
J. Ohlsson and S. Han, *Prioritising Business Processes*, SpringerBriefs in Business Process Management, https://doi.org/10.1007/978-3-319-70398-5_4

and IT was responsible for implementing the "one SECO program". The aim of this program was to create a common understanding and culture with regard to BPM, and to decide on the budget for process improvement projects. The manager faced the following challenges:

(1) Seco Tools stems from the traditional "manufacturing" industry. The company has a rather conservative and strong organization culture.
(2) Business and IT do not share a common understanding of the business. They have a clear vision on process ownership, and quite a different understanding of each other's work. As the CIO/VP said: "*I have the feeling that there were two parties sitting on respective sides of the fence and no common understanding.*"
(3) All businesses ask for improvements in their business areas. But the CIO/VP has limited budgets/resources for executing all projects. He said "*The demand is three times larger than what we could do with existing budgets and resources.*"
(4) The CIO/VP needed clear evidence as well as consensus in prioritizing process improvement projects, to be able to say "no" to other projects. Without transparency and trustworthiness in the decision-making process, the CIO would endanger his position and support in the company.

Configuration of the PCM and the demonstration procedure

(1) The CIO firstly selected 40 processes that were intended for improvement. He then contacted the former CEO, who has worked for 30 years for the company; then he selected the VP in the Asian region, and the global process manager. They together identified 12 out of 40 processes for assessment, including a few simple lower-level processes. The pre-selection was guided by using the PCM.
(2) The CIO and the three managers reviewed and agreed on the core questions in the assessment. Then the three managers further recommended other stake-holders based on their informal network to perform the assessments and interviews. Altogether they selected 20 key stakeholders (both owner and customers of the processes) from different business functions, different countries and from different levels in the organization, i.e., strategic, functional as well as operational. These managers were the CIO/Senior Vice President, Global Distribution Manager, Country Managing Director, Global Process Manager, Director Operations and Human Resources, Quality Manager, Process Owners and Process Improvers.
(3) Interviews with each manager were conducted by involved researchers. In the first part of the interviews the heat map (PAHM) was used. This took about one and half hours. In the second part of the interview the CM assessment was central. This part took about 30 min. The researchers didn't impose personal opinions and kept neutral in the interviews. The interview results were docu-mented and stored in the web tool of the PCM.
(4) Finally, the results from the individual interviews were consolidated, calibrated and coordinated at the end. The evaluation results were presented and discussed

at a Business Process Council meeting where 18 top managers of Seco Tools participated in March 2012. Based on the results, the managers made the following decisions: (1) five processes were prioritized for improvement, including create forecast process; (2) at least two KPIs per process should be published on a regular basis in order to improve process transparency and performance, in order to enhance the "proving" perspective; and (3) the organizational capabilities, e.g., people, culture and IT priorities (reliability, cost, agility, quality) should be in focus for supporting a successful implementation of the prioritized processes.

The results

The demonstration of the PCM to Seco Tools verified that the PCM was usable, effective and efficient. The PCM delivered the expected results in an efficient manner. A significant benefit of using the PCM is that the practitioners can gain a better, and more common, understanding of the processes, their improvement potential and ways to improve them. This builds up a solid foundation for decision-making in prioritising the process improvement initiatives. Furthermore, the company has created a novel way of making decisions by using the PCM. The prioritisation process was transparent, open and trustworthy. This supported the top management in making the right decisions, and created a good "buy in" of the decisions made. Additionally, the top-down social process in using the PCM has been beneficial for the company in eliciting the "intelligence" from the right people, and creating a culture for process management. Therefore, the PCM can enable the avoidance of politics in decision-making for the prioritisation of process initiatives.

In this case, the PCM was used in the context of existing strategies and business models at the respective organisation. In other words, how to deliver their existing products and services in the existing value proposition according to the existing business strategy respectively, as efficiently and effectively as possible, by achieving operational excellence.

4.2   The Pilot Study of the PCM at Ericsson

Ohlsson et al. (2014b) further introduce the PCM with sound theoretical justifications within the research fields of business process management and IT management (see Chap. 2). The paper also present the results from the pilot study of the PCM at Ericsson that was conducted in September–October 2013.

Business context of Ericsson

Ericsson is one of the largest telecommunication companies in the world. After demonstrating the PCM at Seco Tools, Ericsson wanted to evaluate the PCM. The aims of the pilot were: (1) to find an easy and simple method that gives Ericsson a view of the status of its processes and end-to-end flows, as well as creating a common understanding of the problems and improvement potential; (2) to understand the characteristics of the processes and identify the indications for improvements; and, ultimately, (3) to make the decision on whether to include the PCM as a recommended method for process analysis in the Ericsson Business Process (EBP) framework.

The pilot process

The PCM was used for analysing five processes: sales, finance, sourcing, service delivery and supply. They are all level 2 processes at Ericsson. Eleven people were involved in the interviews, and they also evaluated the PCM. Moreover, we interviewed the top manager and the project manager who were in charge of the pilot.

The results

The evaluation of the method is positive. A manager stated: "*in general a good method for the purpose, good results on fairly limited time spent*". The management team and process stakeholders have gained a shared and common understanding of the five processes in the analysis, helping them to identify the critical processes—in this case, the sales process—that need immediate improvement.

The CM (categorisation map) results have imposed the direction to improve the process, which is supportive of decision making. The aims of the pilot have been achieved. This pilot also generated feedback for improving the PCM. (1) the functionality of data retrieval should be improved. The comments document in each perspective/dimension should be able to be retrieved at each process level. (2) The activities of the PCM should give more guidelines on how to select and identify the "right" people for interview. A process analyst commented: "*In order to get results on the method, the selection of interviewees is very important. People need to know the processes and various particularities of the processes*". Then, it is important to cover the various dimensions of the company in the terms of strategic, tactical and operational. For example, it is necessary "*to involve process executors from the operational dimension*". He also pointed out that "*people are cautious and reluctant to comment on other processes*". (3) Ericsson also requires the method to be configurable to achieve a better fit with its business terminology and organizational culture.

In the end, the top management team was quite satisfied with the method and decided to use it for analysing processes at Ericsson.

In this pilot study at Ericsson, the evidence further shows that the PCM is useful and applicable in a real decision-making context. This method is qualitative in nature, and based on subjective human judgement and tactical knowledge from managers and process management practitioners. The PCM activities also create a new way of facilitating and making decisions in prioritizing processes, which is to elicit the "collective intelligence" from the key stakeholders.

4.3   The Large Scale Evaluation of the PCM at Ericsson

Ohlsson et al. (2017) describe the large evaluation of the PCM at Ericsson in 2014–2015. This evaluation involved 55 stakeholders.

Business context and the top management requests

The Ericsson Steering Group (ESG) wanted to understand how their business processes and their capabilities could strategically support its "future business" in their vision of a Networked Society. They wanted answers regarding how Ericsson, in an efficient and effective way, can continue with their profitable businesses in a society that is "connected". In other words: how should the company innovate its strategy and business model to, e.g., sell novel services and products that are delivered in effective and efficient business processes. In this context, the PCM needed to be more configurable to meet the new requirements.

Configuration of the PCM to fit with Ericsson' demands

After a long-time negotiation, the researchers and the managers at Ericsson configured the PCM to meet these demands. The PCM was configured to take into account contextual factors and situational factors that are related to Ericsson's strategic-, process-, organisation-, and environmental- dimensions.

   The five perspectives of the heat map were configured to the business terms that are used by Ericsson, which are: positioning to 'alignment to strategy', relating to 'relation and interface to other stakeholders', preparing to 'capability to execute', implementing to 'actual/required performance', and proving to 'ability to monitor and measure' (see Fig. 4.1).

   As a next step, Ericsson's processes were evaluated using the configured Process Categorisation Method (PCM). The evaluation team was formed by four senior employees, one PCM consultant and one of the researchers. The activities involved

	Core element	Assessing the....
Effectiveness	Alignment to strategy	• Alignment with the **business strategy**, objectives and values
	Relation and interface to other stakeholders	• Relationship, attitudes, roles, risks and rewards of the **stakeholders** exposed to the process
Efficiency	Capability to execute	• Availability and quality of key **capabilities** for working with and in the process
	Actual / required performance	• **Performance** of the process
	Ability to monitor and measure	• Relevance of **measurements**

Fig. 4.1 Specification of PCM heath map topics for Ericsson

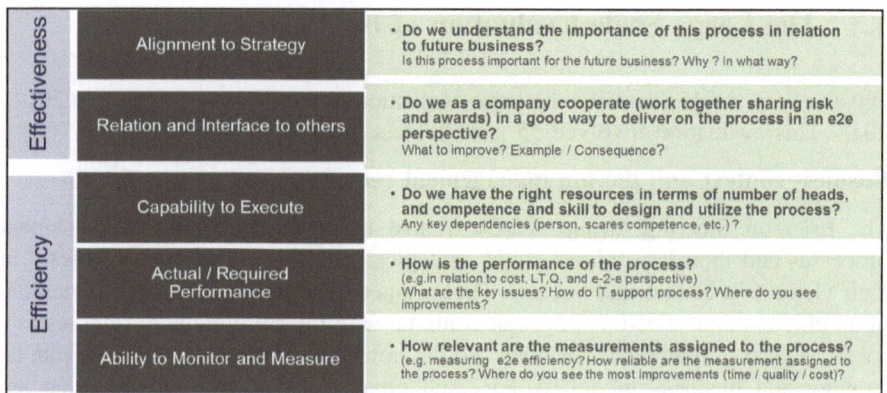

Fig. 4.2 Mapping ESG questions to heath map perspectives

Table 4.1 The questions for the Categorisation Map (CM)

Questions per process	
Is the process customer facing or an internal process? 1–10	Current
Is the process structured or semi structured? 1–10	Current
Is the process differentiating or a commodity process? 1–10	Current
Is the process customer facing or an internal process? 1–10	Future
Is the process structured or semi-structured? 1–10	Future
Is the process differentiating or a commodity process? 1–10	Future

specifying the requirements from the Ericsson Steering Group (ESG) to questions to be used in the steps to generate the heath map (see Fig. 4.2).

For every perspective, the leading principle was defined, for instance, with regard to the positioning perspective, it was important to emphasise that the process should be future-proof; for the relating perspective, the end-to-end of the process was important; for preparing, simplicity was key; with regard to implementing, the involvement of process owners was important. Ultimately, it was crucial to prove that the process would lead to an improved performance.

Ericsson further configured the Categorisation Map from the positioning 'dots' (see Fig. 4.2 both of the as-is and to-be "dots") in the map space to a scale of 1–10, since the ESG expects the quantified results. The questions used in the Categorisation Map are shown in Table 4.1.

The results

Eight business processes (finance, IT, human resources, sales, product management, services, sourcing and supply) were analysed and evaluated at Ericsson by the configured PCM, resulting in new knowledge about which of the processes are most relevant to Ericsson's future business, and which processes and capabilities to build/improve in order to stay successful in future business.

An important insight gained during the implementation of the PCM method within Ericsson was that power struggles became explicit. Power 'politics' will make it more difficult for a company to implement new 'process structures. In practice, most problems are related to the 'governance' and organisational accountability of processes, which are reinforced by Ericsson's complex process structure, with regions, markets and product areas.

After the PCM evaluation. Ericsson is initiating changes.

"*A new governance is in design and planning*" (personal communication from an Ericsson top-manager in June 2016).

In conclusion, the Prioritisation and Categorisation Method (PCM) helped Ericsson to evaluate its processes within its business context and industry environments. The results show that, to realise seamless end-to-end processes in the eight assessed processes, Ericsson has to make a greater effort to improve its process structures, governance and culture to fulfil the needs of future business. The Ericsson Steering Group was satisfied with the insights provided and has decided to train more stakeholders to use the PCM.

References

Ohlsson, J., Han, S., Johannesson, P., Carpenhall, F., & Rusu, L. (2014a). Prioritising business processes improvement initiatives: the Seco tools case. In: M Jarke et al. (Eds.), *Proceedings of 26th International Conference on Advanced Information Systems Engineering* (CAiSE), *Lectures Notes in Computer Science*, LNCS 8484, pp. 256–270. Switzerland: Springer International Publishing.

Ohlsson, J., Han, S., Johannesson, P., & Rusu, L. (2014b). Developing a method for prioritising business process improvement initiatives. In *Proceedings of Pacific Asian Conference on Information Systems* (PACIS), Paper 342, Association of Information Systems (AIS). https://aisel.aisnet.org/pacis2014/342.

Ohlsson, J., Han, S., & Bouwman, H. (2017). The prioritization and categorization method (PCM): An evaluation at Ericsson. *Business Process Management Journal, 23*(2), 377–398.

Chapter 5
Discussions

Abstract The aim of this book is to design and evaluate the artefact—the Prioritisation and Categorisation Method (PCM). This chapter discusses the PCM's contribution to BPM research and practice. The contribution to DSR knowledge is further discussed by articulating the three design principles of the PCM: *design by holistics, design by commitments, and design by explorations.*

Keywords The PCM · Contribution · BPM · Design principles

5.1 The Knowledge Contributions to BPM Research

The Prioritisation and Categorisation Method (PCM) is not only IT-driven, but is also business-driven, in contrast to, for instance, Enterprise Architecture (e.g. Lankhorst et al. 2009; Versteeg and Bouwman 2006) and many Business Process modelling approaches (e.g. Ami and Sommer 2007; Andersson and Johannesson 2009; Curtis et al. 1992; Kettinger et al. 1997; Recker and Rosemann 2009). The case study at Seco Tools indicated that the PCM helped the CIO to communicate with businesses, involve key stakeholders in different business functions in IT decision making, and balance the business need for IT resources. The case study at Ericsson clearly showed that processes that match future business opportunities were crucial reasons for using the PCM in process evaluation and process prioritisation.

Moreover, the PCM can be viewed as a kind of co-creation effort, in which business plays a more important role than IT. This solves one of the problems in Business IT alignment research, where commitment from business is often poor in practice (e.g. Gerow et al. 2014). In the Ericsson case, fifty-five process managers, process owners or process stakeholders were involved in the evaluation of the processes. As 'future business' was the main concern in driving the evaluation, commitments from the business were high. Process management is a 'business' and 'management' practice, which cannot be exclusively dedicated to IT. This co-creation process was also recognised in the case of Seco Tools, which gave greater support for the CIO's decision in the process prioritisation initiatives.

The PCM also distinguishes itself from the top-down Business Architecture approach proposed by Vertseeg and Bouwman (2006). Where strategy serves as a driver for Business Architecture and is based on information from top-level management, and a blueprint for the business architecture is made. In addition to considering the top-management's requirements, the PCM is able to involve the managers/owners of the processes from different levels within an organisation in defining their process domain as well as the alignment between the processes, business and strategy. The results of the PCM are aggregated by collecting opinions and tactical knowledge from the stakeholders and process owners, in other words, the people who know the operation and performance of a particular process. As a result, decisions are made based on this 'collective intelligence' or 'collective reflection-in-action', which can be called a 'bottom-up' approach to managing processes. This intelligence provides direct indications for the redistribution of resources and the acquisition of dynamic BPM capabilities for business purposes. As such, the PCM introduces a transparent and democratic procedure for process management decision-making, as it provides evidence of why the decisions were made, and it shows why such decisions have been chosen.

Moreover, the evaluation of business processes using the PCM has raised awareness among managers of what to think, what to do and how to understand the processes in their entirety, and not as 'separate' processes that they are owned. As a result, the awareness creates a supportive culture for new business process modelling. People are more prepared for possible changes due to changes in strategy. People are one of the key elements of strategic BPM (Rosemann and vom Brocke 2010), in that 'people' implement and invoke in each other's presence to promote a particular action to achieve a strategic purpose, which means that it is important to fully consider people's role in strategic planning and BPM activities (e.g. Ackoff 1994; MacLean and MacIntosh 2015).

Compared to other holistic approaches, e.g. Archimate (Lankhorst et al. 2009) or Aris (Scheer 1998), and various maturity models (e.g., Röglinger et al. 2012; Rosemann and de Bruin 2005; Weber et al. 2004), the PCM is easy to use, simple and can yield results within a short period of time. The demonstration at Seco Tools was completed in one month. After configuring the questions and focusing on the most important aspects that interested Ericsson, the evaluation of the eight core processes was completed in three months, which would not be possible by, for example, applying maturity models to determine where to improve process capabilities. Speed and timing of decision-making are becoming increasingly important in a digital world (Bharadwaj et al. 2013). Faster and more effective decisions are needed to survive in the turbulent economic environment that companies face nowadays.

To conclude, the PCM provides a more explorative approach to Business Process Management, taking into account the business processes in business contexts, business cultures, governance and governance mechanisms, related to the availability of resources and capabilities, or the need to make the latter available.

Because no comparison has been conducted between the PCM and other possible methods of process improvement in the empirical case studies, we lack the empirical evidences to claim that the PCM is more appropriate than other BPM methods that serve the same purpose, i.e. prioritising and categorising business processes. The theoretical argumentation of comparing the PCM with other methods (see Lehnert et al. 2016), as we discussed earlier, can support the argument that the PCM is a satisfactory solution to address process prioritisation problems in various contexts. More importantly, the collected empirical evidence shows that the PCM helps to solve problems, offers high quality results in a flexible and efficient way, it is appreciated by practitioners and it can be applied in real business practices. The method is configurable, flexible and adaptable. Furthermore, the empirical cases show the evidences that the PCM foster the key capabilities of explorative BPM, which are aimed to craft process visions by involving relevant stakeholders, customers, and employees to explore how to make a desired further state; and to identify the opportunities that create new business and revenue (e.g. Ericsson evaluation).

5.2 The Design Principles for the PCM

In this section, we discuss the PCM contribution to DSR knowledge. First, the contribution is articulated as "invention" based on the DSR knowledge contribution framework (Gregor and Hevner 2013). Second, the design principles for the PCM is discussed based on our critical reflections.

Reflecting on the research results and the entire six years that have encompassed this Design Science Research, we realised that we should abstract the nascent design theory, the design principles for the PCM that can be shared with other designers in solving similar ill-structured problems in the context of process management. Gregor and Hevner (2013) define this kind of design knowledge contribution as fundamental truths or propositions that can serve as a design knowledge base for others. The three design principles have been elucidated based on the total experience and critical reflections of this research endeavour from both theoretical and practical perspectives (see Table 5.1).

The underlying assumption for the three design principles is the theory that organisations and firms are social systems, and thus should be designed and managed as such. Further, many of the problems that managers handle in organisations are open-ended, circular and ill-structured. The social model conceptualises organisations as social systems that should be viewed as a part of a larger purposeful system as well as a system with purposeful parts. It focuses on both the functions of the parts in the whole and of the whole in the larger containing system of which it is a part. Therefore, it can yield an understanding of both the behaviour of the parts and the whole.

Table 5.1 The three design principles for the PCM

Principle #1: **Design by holistics**	Organisations as social systems require a holistic design approach, which means that the more parts of the system and levels of it that plan simultaneously and interdependently, the better. The practice of management should create a true whole and harmonise decisions and actions
Principle #2: **Design by commitments**	Management should be centred on "conversations for action". Success cannot be attributed to a decision made by a particular actor, but only to the collective performance. Knowledge and understanding arise from a shared background of actions. Unstructured or judgemental decision-making is dependent largely on a manger's intuitive skills, the feeling of the phenomena, tacit knowledge and reflection-in-action
Principle #3: **Design by explorations**	A solution space is co-evolved with a problem space. "Designing without final goals" where design goals are a function that motivates activities that in turn generates new goals. A designed artefact serves as a starting point for new possibilities and actions

Principle #1: Design by holistics

The principle of design by holistics specifies that design for solving ill-structured problems, e.g. process prioritisation and process innovation, should make as many parts of the organisation interactively involved in the design process as possible in order to create a true whole and to harmonise decisions and actions.

When managing ill-structured problems in the contemporary business environment, managers not only have to manage their own domain or function, but also other domains and functions that contribute to the whole economic performance of the organisation (Drucker 2007). If they focus strictly on their domain or function, there is a high risk of sub-optimisation and "the whole" becomes un-coordinated. This is valid for all sub-systems (parts or functions) in a firm. More and more organisations consist of many knowledge intensive processes, which makes it difficult to delegate any problems with clear instructions to different management levels. Furthermore, the board and the top-management level in an organisation needs the planning input from their different business functions from every level of the organisation. Therefore, the involvement of managers from every level and by every function is vital to achieve a holistic view of the problems at hand, and make decisions that can benefit the organisation as a whole, and not just one business domain or function.

In the design-process of the PCM, practitioners such as CIOs and business process owners from various big companies in Sweden had participated in all of the DSR activities, from the problem formulation to the demonstration and evaluation. They hold positions at different levels of an organisation, as well as being responsible for various business domains. Because these practitioners possess professional knowledge and reflection of their experiences in their daily management practice, their contributions to the design of the PCM are enormous. Through the hermeneutics process of interpreting the divergent professional knowledge, the holistic perspective, thus it is embodied in the output of the design. This, to a great extent, increases the relevance and applicability of the designed artefacts.

The demonstration and evaluation of the PCM in the empirical case studies further enforced the holistic perspective of the design. The PCM approaches process management using the interactive planning principles proposed by Ackoff (1994). The PCM has proven to be efficient. The selection process of the stakeholders in the PCM is explorative in its nature. Both formal and informal managers and stakeholders at all levels of the organisation and from every functions were involved in the process assessments and the decision-making for the process prioritisation. As expressed by a CIO in an evaluation of the PCM (Seco Tools):

"It is very important to choose the right interviewees. They should not only be from the management group, but they should also be from a more heterogonous group of key stakeholders, informal leaders in the organisation, such as individuals who have no formal leadership but have a strong position and great knowledge of the business. The number should be manageable, given the size of the business with a decent coverage of the business areas. You have to adopt the method to your own business".

Or, as mentioned by a manager in another PCM evaluation (Ericsson):

"The evaluation has made every manager involved aware and think more holistically about processes as a whole, and not focusing on only one process that a manager owns. They start to think and understand that the processes should service all kinds of business areas that Ericsson aims for, not only one business area".

Principle #2: Design by commitments

The principle of design by commitments specifies that design for solving an ill-structured problem in organisations should create conversations within the situated contexts, and make the design process a collective reflection-in-action for the key stakeholders.

Management decision-making is limited by bounded rationality. For ill-structured problems, the managers' own intuitive and judgemental skills have approved fundamental influences on the decisions made. However, success cannot be attributed to a decision made by a particular actor, but only to the collective performance. Knowledge and understanding arise from a shared background of actions. The knowledge cannot be shared via a one-way communication, the knowledge and learning is actually "made by doing" or in actual dialogue between stakeholders with different backgrounds and pre-knowledge of certain domains. Therefore, management should be centred on "conversations for action" and create networks of commitments in the design process when solving ill-structured problems.

In the design-process of the PCM, the practitioners involved had been engaged in continuous negotiations or "conversations for action" to reach a common understanding of the PCM, its two models, and the perspectives and dimensions that are represented in the two models. In this dynamic iterative process, ideas and theories have been presented, debated and interpreted together with the engaged stakeholders until a construct or artefact was designed. Then, the particular artefact was tested in different settings, both in real business settings, cases and in other plenums. The design was iterated several times by further negotiation and debate until it has been considered as "good enough" for its final evaluation. The advantage of this approach is that the committed practitioners easily accept the artefact and also develop a true belief that it can be used in real cases and settings.

When the committed practitioners tested the PCM in their own organisations, this principle design by commitment was further implemented in the process assessments. In the cases, we have seen that business stakeholders and managers become engaged when they are involved with the PCM. They become both the consumer of knowledge from the PCM, and the contributor of knowledge to the problem in the scope (process prioritisation). This engagement is important because it is the fundament for action, e.g. in designing the PCM, in evaluating and using the PCM in real businesses, as well as in decision-making based on this collective manner. As the CIO from Seco Tools reflected:

"The *method is a tremendous help to me, in that it creates, together with the management board, a common picture regarding our as-is state and to-be state. It was a foundation, where we could agree which process works well and which does worse. This consensus was not present at all before we did this demonstration. We know where to assign our resources to the prioritised process. The processes that work fine can wait*".

He continued with: "*The method helped us to decide what, where in the processes the improvements should take place, but then, the how is the next question that the method can indicate. Should we go for a larger change project or implement an existing process with everyday business operations through a small adjustment?*"

The CIO explains further that: "*By using the method in the decision-making process, I took help from the ones that have spent their entire career in the business; those who know how things really work... I got a sense of what is important at present, and what I should do next*".

Principle #3: Design by explorations

The principle of design by explorations specifies that design for solving ill-structured problems should be explorative rather than exploitative, especially for organisations that operate in dynamic environments. Firms that act in dynamic environments have to learn by continuous interactions, both internally and in dialogues with their environments and contexts, if not, they will not survive (Beer 1979). The design exploration of ill-structured problem posits a continuous, circular and open-ended process (Maher et al. 1996). Simon (1996) defines this as "Designing without final goals". Design goals are a function that motivates activities which in turn generates new goals. A designed artefact serves as a starting point for new possibilities and actions. For the ill-structured problem solving situations, we get satisfactory solutions rather than optimised designs (Simon 1996).

The design activities of the PCM demonstrate the significance of the explorative approach. In the beginning of the design process, the design problem was formulated and limited as IT managers had difficulties in making and executing decisions in regards to supporting business activities and to prioritising processes to improve business values. The design of the PCM was iterated for more than 2 years before the prototype was demonstrated at Seco Tools. Several collaboration workshops were arranged in order to abstract the managers' professional knowledge in the method design. The success story gained at Seco Tools did give the first evidence of the usefulness of the PCM in solving the problem of process prioritisation. However, when business environments become more dynamic, uncertain and complex, organisations face tremendous challenges from digital technologies, or disruptive technologies. This posed new problems in the problem domain for process improvement and process management in dynamic environments. The evaluation of the PCM at Ericsson has brought new evidence that the PCM has to be explored to solve the problems that concern processes for successful future businesses. In these design exploration activities, we argue that the PCM is co-evolved with its problem spaces, to be exact, from an IT driven process prioritisation problem, to process innovation in a dynamic environment, and to process improvement for achieving future business. The empirical studies provide strong evidence of success from this explorative process.

Thus, this research has not been finalised with "the solution to the problem". And this will according to the design by explorations principle continue the explorative process. With the co-evolution of the problem and solution spaces, this explorative process is open-ended. Ill-structured problems cannot be understood completely and solved immediately, thus a solution can only be designed based on the limited scope of problem formulation. In the research for the ill-structured problem solving situations, we get satisfactory solutions rather than optimised designs. Thus, the PCM is a satisfactory solution at this point in time. It is a starting point for continuous exploration to find further satisfactory solutions to the continuous evolution of problems that arise in the business contexts of most firms today.

BPM contains many ill-structured and complex problems. Explorative BPM has emerged as a new research direction to address these problems. In practice, managers and stakeholders should make continuous designs based on their limited understanding of the problem domains. Exploration is the crucial principle for the design process in these contexts.

5.3   The Contributions to BPM Practice

Today, many companies act in a fast changing and turbulent business environment, and should aim to implement changes that are based on faster and more effective decision-making. The PCM can provide a transparent and democratic decision-making procedure, and it can yield high-quality results within a short period of time, generating a shared understanding of process improvements and potential changes. Investment in process improvements or re-design should not only focus on process models or IT, but it should also look towards cultivating a supportive culture and motivated employees who are keen to change and adapt.

The PCM has also demonstrated how evaluation of processes can include organisational factors and environmental variables that organisations are most interested in understanding, especially when improving current business and creating future business. There is no 'one-size-fits all model' that can be applied here. Each company should configure their own PCM to fit its business contingencies and contexts, which means the PCM should not be seen as a method to solve every process improvement problem, but as an inspiration for determining an appropriate evaluation for a company's business needs.

Table 5.2 The PCM contribution to good BPM Practice

Principles of good BPM practice	The PCM contributions
Principle of context—awareness	The PCM is easy to configure to fit into an organisational context. Thus, business contingencies and environmental factors can be considered in process evaluation and process improvement or redesign
Principle of continuity	The PCM facilitates a continuous process evaluation based on an organisation's needs
Principle of enablement	The PCM helps companies to create capabilities to improve processes, and categorise resources and capabilities that they may need to realise future, as well as current, business
Principle of holism	The PCM is theoretically built upon a holistic approach, and does not focus only on IT, process modelling or methods. Strategy, governance, people and culture, together with IT and models are considered
Principle of institutionalisation	The PCM is configurable to analyse 'which processes within what context'. As a result, organisational structure is embedded in the PCM
Principle of involvement	Using the PCM requires all of the process stakeholders to actively participate in process evaluation, resulting in a democratic and transparent evaluation that can benefit everybody
Principle of joint understanding	The PCM creates a shared understanding among key stakeholders who participate in process evaluations. In interactive evaluation sessions, a common understanding of the processes is generated naturally
Principle of purpose	The results of the PCM serves as the foundation for top-management decision-making regarding companies' process improvement and strategic movement towards the to-be situation
Principle of simplicity	The PCM is easy to use. Satisfactory results can be obtained in a relatively short time
Principle of technology appropriation	The use of the PCM in process evaluation is supported by a web-based tool in the cloud. The tool can document all of the evaluation interactions, comments, and aggregate/visualise the results. Although for security reasons, companies, like Ericsson, would develop their own tool for supporting the use of the PCM

Finally, the PCM leads to potential changes in process governance, both internally and externally, especially if the company operates in a dynamic environment. The PCM may make the internal 'power politics' explicitly, which can help leaders to find where resistance is coming from and help them to deal with change resistance efficiently. Moreover, the PCM can help companies to identify a strong governance position of those processes in their value network in order to create and capture business values.

In Sweden the PCM has been demonstrated and evaluated in more than 15 cases. In some of the cases, consultant firms have supported the PCM practice. Two of the empirical cases (e.g. Seco Tools and Ericsson) have been published with the permission of the organisations involved. BPM analytics companies and management consultants are educated and trained to use the method. So far the method has been appreciated for its novelty and its complementary abilities for other more mechanistically and analytically designed methods and models.

In conclusion, the PCM embodies a high degree of relevance to business practice. In addition to the research collaboration/co-design in all of the design activities with the practitioners through an engaged scholarship approach, Dr. Jens Ohlsson's professional knowledge has also played a significant role in designing and evaluating the PCM. This also increases the relevance of the research to practice (see Preface; Klein and Rowe 2008). In Table 5.2, we abstract the contribution of the PCM to practice based on the ten principles of good BPM practice (vom Brocke et al. 2014).

References

Ackoff, R. L. (1994). *The democratic corporation: A radical prescription for recreating corporate America and rediscovering success.* Oxford: Oxford University Press.

Ami, T., & Sommer, R. (2007). Comparison and evaluation of business process modelling and management tools. *International Journal of Services and Standards, 3*(2), 249–261.

Andersson, B., & Johannesson, P. (2009). Aligning goals services through goal and business modelling. *Information System E-Business Management, 7*(2), 143–169.

Beer, S. (1979). *The heart of enterprise* (Vol. 2). London: Wiley.

Bharadwaj, A., El Sawy, O. A., Pavlou, P. A., & Venkatraman, N. V. (2013). Digital business strategy: Toward a next generation of insights. *MIS Quarterly, 37*(2), 471–482.

Curtis, W., Kellner, M. I., & Over, J. (1992). Process modelling. *Communication of the ACM, 35* (9), 75–90.

Drucker, P. F. (2007). *The practice of management.* Elsevier Ltd.

Gerow, J. E., Grover, V., Thatcher, J. B., & Roth, P. L. (2014). Looking toward the future of IT-Business strategic alignment through the past: A meta-analysis. *MIS Quarterly, 38*(4), 1059–1085.

Gregor, S., & Hevner, A. R. (2013). Positioning and presenting design science research for maximum impact. *MIS Quarterly, 37*(2), 335–337.

Kettinger, W. J., Teng, J. T. C., & Guha, S. (1997). Business process change: A study of methodologies, methods, and tools. *MIS Quarterly, 21*(1), 55–80.

Klein, H., & Rowe, F. (2008). Marshalling the professional experience of doctoral student: A contribution to the practical relevance debate. *MIS Quarterly, 32*(4), 675–686.

Lankhorst, M. M., Proper, H. A., & Jonkers, H. (2009). The architecture of the archimate language. In T. Halpin, et al. (Eds.) *BPMDS 2009 and EMMSAD 2009, lecture notes in business information processing* (pp. 367–380). Berlin: Springer.

Lehnert, M., Linhart, A., & Röglinger, M. (2016). Value-based process project portfolio management: Integrated planning of BPM capability development and process improvement. *Business Research, 9*(2), 377–419.

MacLean, D., & MacIntosh, R. (2015). Planning reconsidered: Paradox, poetry and people at the edge of strategy. *European Management Journal, 33*(2), 72–78.

Maher, M. L., Poon, J., & Boulanger, S. (1996). Formalising design exploration as co-evolution: A combined gene approach. In J. Gero, et al. (Eds.), *Advances in formal design methods for CAD* (pp. 3–30). Dordrecht: Springer Science & Business Media.

Recker, J. C., & Rosemann, M. (2009). Teaching business process modelling: Experiences and recommendations. *Communications of the Association for Information Systems, 24*(1), 379–394.

Rosemann, M., & de Bruin, T. (2005). Towards a business process management maturity model. In *Proceedings of the 13th European Conference on Information Systems (ECIS)* (pp. 521–532).

Rosemann, M., & vom Brocke, J. (2010). The six core elements of business process management. In vom Brocke, J., & Rosemann, M. (Eds.), *Handbook on business process management* (Vol. 1, pp. 107–122). Berlin: Springer.

Röglinger, M., Pöppelbuß, J., & Becker, J. (2012). Maturity models in business process management. *Business Process Management Journal, 18*(2), 328–346.

Scheer, A. W. (1998). *ARIS—business process frameworks* (3rd ed.). Berlin: Springer.

Simon, H. A. (1996). *The sciences of the artificial* (3rd ed.). Cambridge: MIT Press.

Versteeg, G., & Bouwman H., (2006). Business architecture: A new paradigm to relate business strategy to ICT. *Information Systems Frontiers, 8*(2), 91–102.

vom Brocke, J., Schmiedel, T., Recker, J., Trkman, P., Mertens, W., & Viaene, S. (2014). Ten principles of good business process management. *Business Process Management Journal, 20*(4), 530–548.

Weber, C. V., Curtis, B., & Gardiner, T. (2004). Business process maturity model (BPMM), Version 1, www. omg.org/spec/BPMM/1.0/. Last accessed January 3, 2013.

Chapter 6
Conclusions

Abstract This chapter revisits the main results of the book, highlight the key contributions of the PCM. Limitations and future research is elaborated at the end.

Keywords PCM · BPM

6.1 The Main Results Revisited

This research designed and evaluated a new context-aware, easy-to-use and holistic method for BPM, the Prioritisation and Categorisation Method (PCM). The demonstration conducted at Seco Tools and the evaluation at Ericsson showed that the PCM can support companies when prioritising their processes. By using the PCM, the tacit knowledge of process stakeholders was collected and served as the foundation for any decision-making with regards to process prioritisation, and the vision of the future for the process as well as future business. The PCM also introduced a transparent and democratic procedure for process management decision-making, it provided evidence of why the decisions were made, and what motivated them. Top management, both at Seco Tools and Ericsson, was satisfied with the insights that were gained through the PCM demonstration and evaluation. At Ericsson, the PCM was included in their enterprise business management framework and more process stakeholders were trained to use the PCM.

6.2 The Research Contributions

The PCM contributes knowledge to IS research in two areas. First, the knowledge contributions to BPM research, which include the PCM as a novel method for exploring process innovation and prioritisation, as well for fostering the key capability of explorative BPM. Second, the knowledge contributions to Design Science Research, which include the PCM as an invention, empirical instantiations,

© The Author(s) 2018

J. Ohlsson and S. Han, *Prioritising Business Processes*, SpringerBriefs in Business Process Management, https://doi.org/10.1007/978-3-319-70398-5_6

and the three design principles for the PCM. We summarise the contributions briefly in the following.

The PCM contribution to BPM research:

- The PCM is both business and IT-driven.
- The PCM can be viewed as a kind of co-creation effort, in which business plays a more important role than IT.
- The PCM supports decisions to be made on the basis of a 'collective intelligence'. The PCM is able to involve the managers/owners of the processes from different levels within an organisation in defining their process domain as well as the alignment between the processes, business and strategy.
- The PCM raises awareness among managers about what to think, what to do and how to understand the processes in their entirety, and not as 'separate' processes.
- The PCM is easy to use, simple and can yield results within a short period of time.

The PCM contribution to DSR knowledge:

- The PCM is considered as an invention and a novel method for supporting decision-making in process prioritisation.
- The design principles for the PCM: design by holistics, design by commitments, and design by exploration are a significant contribution to DSR knowledge. The design theory for the PCM is a nascent theory that can guide others to design methods for process management.
- Because the practitioners' reflections and professional knowledge have shaped the design of the PCM significantly, the artefact has embodied a high level of relevance to business problems. Thus, the artefact shows genuine applicability in businesses.

To conclude, the PCM provides a more explorative approach to Business Process Management, taking into account business processes in business contexts, business cultures, governance and governance mechanisms, related to the availability of resources and capabilities. The PCM is able to be configured to fit organisations' business contingencies. Moreover, the research contributes significant knowledge to Design Science Research. The three design principles for the PCM exhibit possible generalisability to different contexts.

6.3 Limitations and Future Research

It is worth mentioning that the research presented in this book is based on the design and cases within specific cultural and organisational settings (Sweden and Swedish organisations), in which management has its emphasis on empowerment, teamwork and consensus-based decision making (Birkinshaw 2002). The results can be argued not necessarily be generalisable to other cultural, business and industry settings. However, we argue that by virtue of explorative BPM, organisations need to configure the PCM in consideration of their own processes and business contingencies to explore and fulfil their unique process management purposes. This task is more crucial for businesses operating in dynamic environments. Furthermore, it has not been proven that the PCM can support a company in becoming more successful in exploring its BPM by generating new revenue streams based on decisions and prioritisations directly from the PCM.

Future research is worthy of exploring the following questions with regards to Design Science Research and the design of collaborative decision and management methods, as well as improvements to the PCM.

- How could DSR be categorised (with the purpose of supporting researchers and practitioners with common references, for example, using applicable DSR methods to conduct practice-oriented research). The value of doing this research would contribute more relevant judgement to the different types of DSR methods. This could be done by defining different approaches of DSR; such as explorative DSR, which would be circular and interactive; and exploitative DSR, which would be more linear and nominal.
- Designing more pragmatic methods for process innovation (based on the three design principles: design by holistics, design by commitments and design by explorations). This would be relevant because of the digitalisation and innovation issues that address most industries and organisations today.
- Using the PCM for evaluating units of analysis other than processes. Doing this type of research would be relevant because of the contexts for making decisions regarding other objects, other than business processes, that inhabit similar criteria, e.g. ill-structured problem situations and soft system characteristics. This research can be done by making the PCM even more configurable and also implementing it with other units of analysis, e.g. project portfolio objects, capabilities and/or product and services, the principles of the PCM can be used in other types of decision contexts.
- Using data from the PCM to create patterns regarding good practice in different areas and contexts, such as industry sectors. This type of research could be relevant to support companies regarding "the next steps" after process assessments by the PCM, i.e. how to work with certain improvement capabilities for identified process problems by certain types of patterns. For example, where would lean-approaches suit and adaptive case management approaches fit to improve a process, this should also be contextually driven. It should not only be linked to improvement methods as mentioned above, but also linked to patterns regarding the degree of change, e.g. radical changes regarding governance or organisational structures for certain processes. This research could probably be conducted by more exploitative research approaches such as a quantitative analysis of the PCM repository, comparing data from different cases and combining these with literature studies and cases identifying similarities to generate patterns.

- Balancing exploitation and exploration in companies is challenging. This has been discussed and debated in organisation science and management science (e.g. O'Reilly and Tushman 2013; Raisch et al. 2009). An exploration approach is quite new for the BPM community. Although this research argued the importance of exploration in designing the process prioritisation method, the ambidextrous capabilities related to exploitation and exploration are not addressed. This is a promising avenue for future research to continuously explore solutions for prioritisations.

References

Birkinshaw, J. (2002). The art of Swedish management. *Business Strategy Review, 13*(2), 11–19.

O'Reilly, C. A., & Tushman, M. L. (2013). Organizational ambidexterity: Past, present and future. Available at http://www.hbs.edu/faculty/Publication%20Files/O'Reilly%20and%20Tushman% 20AMP%20Ms%20051413_c66b0c53-5fcd-46d5-aa16-943eab6aa4a1.pdf. Last accessed on October 9, 2016.

Raisch, S., Birkinshaw, J., Probst, G., & Tushman, M. L. (2009). Organizational ambidexterity: Balancing exploitation and exploration for sustained performance. *Organization Science, 20* (4), 685–695.

Appendix
The Web-Based Tool for the PCM

This appendix, presenting the web-based tool for the PCM, is divided in three sections; (1) How to configure and set-up an assessment, (2) how the tool facilitates and supports interviews, and (3) how the tool facilitates and supports decision by aggregations of results.

How to Configure and Set-Up Assessments

The first activity in the tool is to create and set up an assessment. See Fig. A.1.

The next step is to document the business structure, by either modelling the process architecture or inserting the process structure based on existing documentation. The PCM is engaged in the assessments from Level 1 to Level 3, which are the core corporate processes (Level 1), process areas (Level 2) and main processes (Level 3) (Fig. A.2).

The next activity is to select the processes (units of analysis) that should be in scope for the PCM.

The method and tool also includes configuration ability, where the configuration can be iterated with focal stakeholders to suit the specific preferences of the respective company or organisation. Configuration can be done at a language level and at a question level. The tool has a pool of questions. If the company or organisation wants to create their own questions, new questions can be formulated in the tool. A quality assurance procedure, where the researcher accepts the question, has to be followed before the question can be included in the existing question pool for each perspective. For efficiency purpose no more than two questions are recommended for each perspective (Figs. A.3, A.4 and A.5).

© The Author(s) 2018
J. Ohlsson and S. Han, *Prioritising Business Processes*, SpringerBriefs in Business Process Management, https://doi.org/10.1007/978-3-319-70398-5

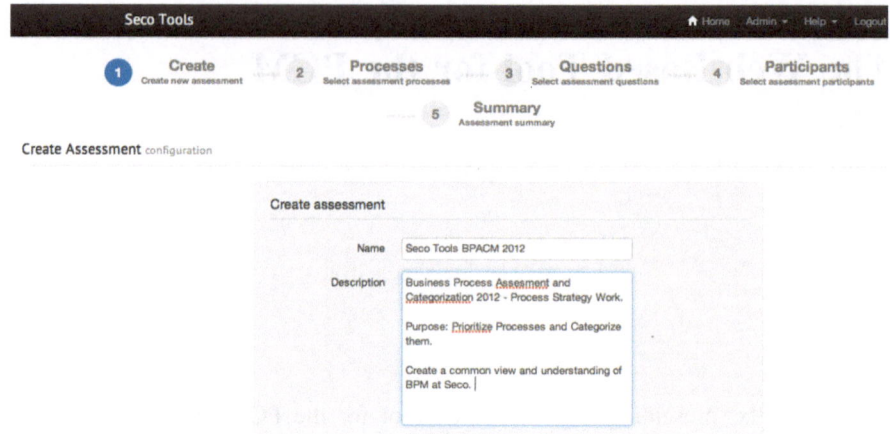

Fig. A.1 Example of the PCM tool in the Seco Case

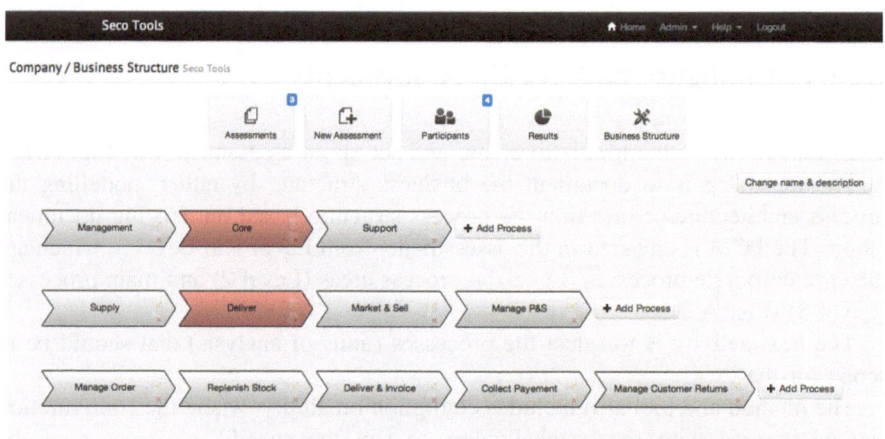

Fig. A.2 Example of the company business structure in the PCM tool of the Seco Case

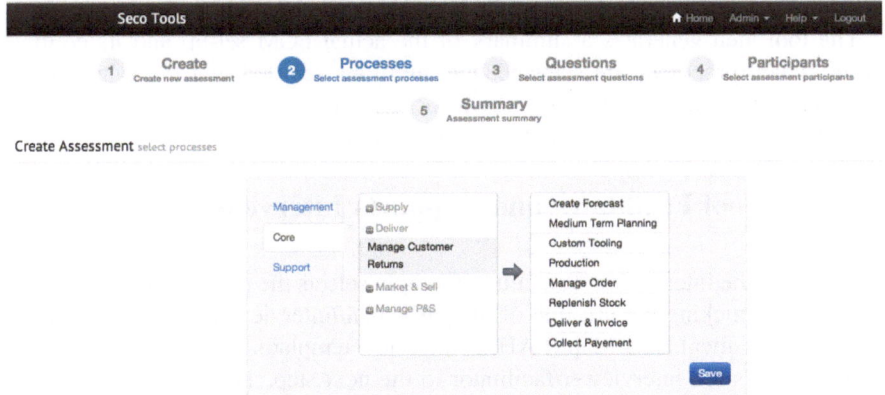

Fig. A.3 Example of the process selection activity in the PCM

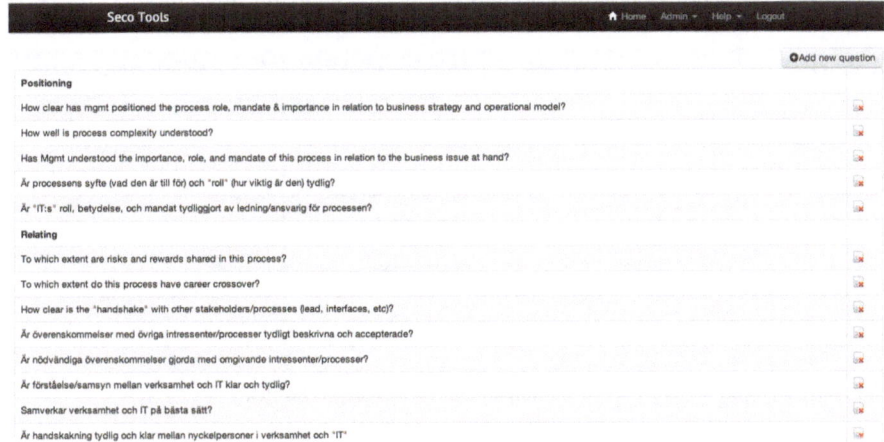

Fig. A.4 Example configuration of question in the PCM

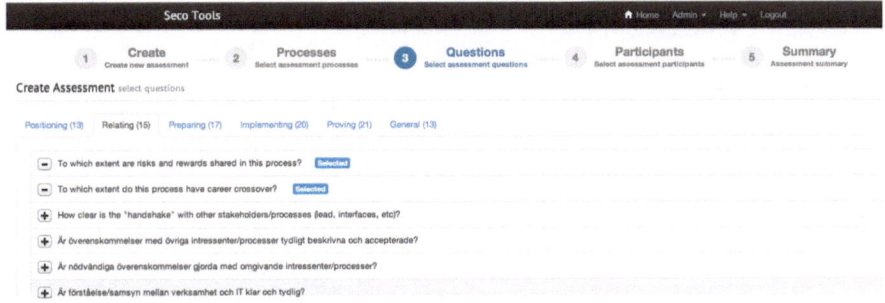

Fig. A.5 Example selection of questions in the PCM

The next activity is to select participants/interviewees (Fig. A.6).

The tool then generates a summary of the actual PCM set-up and its configuration, which processes are selected, the questions selected and the selected participants. Selection of participant can also be done iteratively e.g. by asking for relevant interviewees after an interview (Fig. A.7).

How the Tool Facilitates and Supports Interviews

In this phase the interviewer or facilitator simply selects the participant and starts an interview by clicking the url: link of the participant/interviewee. The tool starts the Process Assessment Heat Map (PAHM) interview template. When the form is filled the tool guides the interviewer/facilitator to the next step. The PAHM can also be completed by a participant, without facilitation by an interviewer (this has not yet been evaluated.) Comments can and should also be added for each question. A typical comment for quality assurance of the selected colour is to ask the respondent for a practical example and reason for choosing the colour (Fig. A.8).

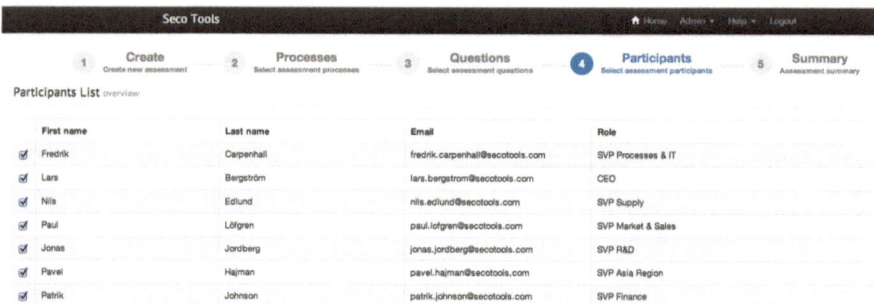

Fig. A.6 Example of selection of participants/interviewees in the PCM

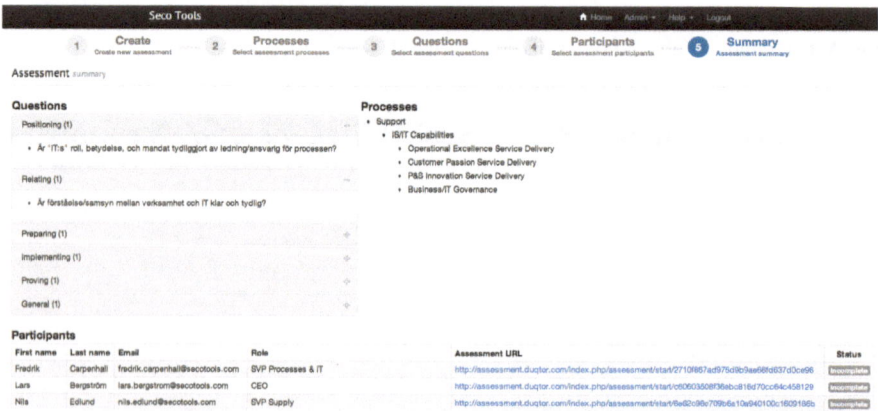

Fig. A.7 Example of a summary with selected processes, questions and participants in PCM

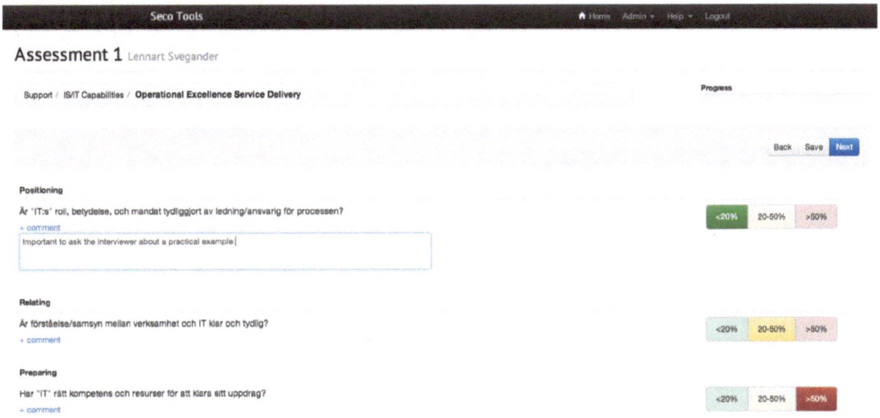

Fig. A.8 Example of the PAHM interview template PCM

When the PAHM is ready the tool starts the CM (Categorisation Map) interview template. (If the PCM is configured without the CM it will not start). For CM, See example in the CM figure further below. The interviewer or interviewee drag the dots: As-Is and To-Be, places them on the CM and make comments. The CM is constructed as a six-cell grid in two dimensions rather than a cube in three dimensions. The reasons for this design choice are that: (1) the visualisation of results in two dimensions is easy to understand, and (2) a process that has the characteristics of being common and informal, independent from the question if it is a back or front process *ideally* should not exist. If such a process exists in reality, then A* is documented in the comment field to indicate this instance.

The **differentiating dimension** assesses the degree to which a process is superior to analogous processes of competitors, thereby differentiating the value proposition of the organisation (scale: differentiating to common). **Sample question:** Does the process in scope differentiate your company versus your competitors? Does the process in scope perform more poorly than for your competitors?

The **formality dimension** assesses the degree to which a process is strictly managed, repeatable, predictable, automatable, and involves applications rather than people (scale: formal to informal). **Sample question**: Does the process in scope reside in tacit knowledge? How strictly is the process in scope managed? How much of the process in scope is performed in an unstructured way? How much of the process is performed with manual work?

The **governance positioning** in the value network makes it clear whether process governance is positioned at the front-end or at the back-end (scale: back to front). **Sample question:** Does the process under governance concern suppliers, consumers or other internal or external actors? Where is the governance of the process positioned?

The tool shows the status of total PCM instances in the summary view, which shows interviews that has been completed (See Fig. A.9).

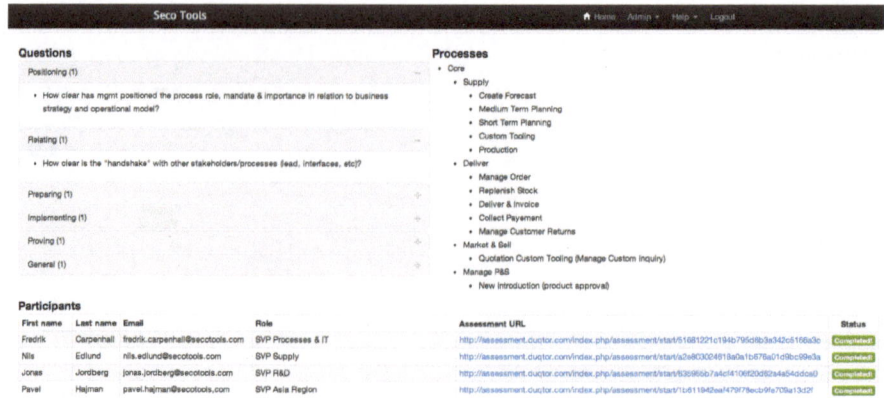

Fig. A.9 Example of summary and which interviews that has been completed

How the Tool Facilitates and Supports Decision by Aggregations of Results

An important feature of the PCM web-based tool is its aggregation of the results of the interviews. The aggregated models are used in the management meetings and workshops to facilitate the discussions and decisions to be made. Below are examples of aggregated models PAHM and PCM generated by the PCM web-based tool, by clicking the result at the bottom of the company page the tool generates the aggregated views. These can be generated on both individual and group levels with several interviewees included (Fig. A.10).

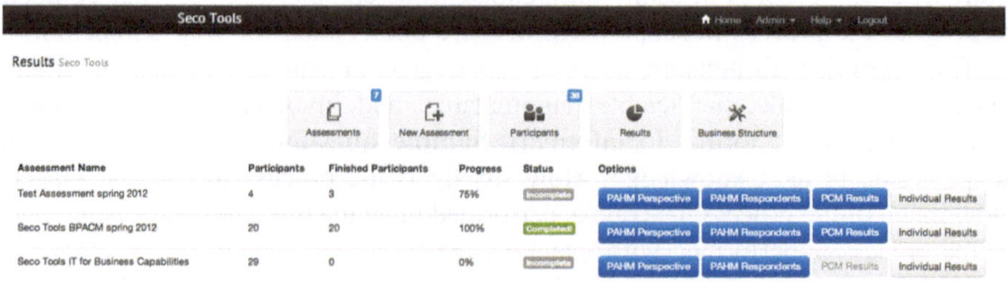

Fig. A.10 Example of result aggregations that can be generated